THE AI WORK WEEK

ASHLEY GROSS

THE AI WORK WEEK

Cut Hours, Automate Busywork, and Focus on What Actually Matters

WILEY

Published by John Wiley & Sons, Inc., Hoboken, New Jersey.

Library of Congress Cataloging-in-Publication Data has been applied for:

ISBN 9781394378210 (Paperback)
ISBN 9781394378241 (oBook)
ISBN 9781394378227 (ePub)
ISBN 9781394378234 (ePDF)

Cover Design: Wiley

SKY10162375_071426

Contents

Acknowledgments *ix*

1 FAQ **1**
Why People Are Nervous About Using AI at Work 2
What Risks Should I Actually Be Thinking About? 4
What Should I Be Automating? 6
How Do I Prevent AI From Consuming My Life? 8

2 Assess Your Current Workflow **11**
The True Cost 11
Identifying Inefficiencies in Your Workday 17
What Tasks Waste the Most Time at Work 20
Mapping Your Weekly Workflow 24
Which Work Activities Should Never Be Automated 30

3 Identifying Automation Opportunities **35**
Repetitive Tasks AI Can Automate at Work 36
Async Team Updates Without Rewriting Your Own Brain 37
Treating Meetings as Inputs Instead of Obligations 39
First Drafts Without Starting From Scratch 40
Turning Existing Work Into Decks You Can Refine 42
Deciding What Should Be Automated First 44
AI Automation for Knowledge Workers 54
Instant Project and Decision History 59
Faster Onboarding for New Hires 61
Client Account Briefing in One Question 62

4 Multiplication Effect **67**
Becoming a Multiplier 71
Three-Phase Reduction 78
Perfectionist's Paradox 94
Build It Ugly, Fix It Later 103

5 Maximize Efficiency Gains **107**
Productivity at a New Baseline 111
The Tech Stack Marriage Audit 113
The Marketing Tech Stack 116
The Sales Tech Stack 116
The Customer Experience Tech Stack 120
Three Decisions That Close the Gap 128

6 AI ROI **135**
Experiment: AI Lead Scoring and Routing 138
Experiment: AI-Assisted Deal Prioritization and Follow-up 141
Experiment: AI-Driven Upsell Triggers from Product Usage 143
Experiment: Cross-Departmental Signal Routing 146
From Proof Points to a Portfolio 146
Decision Rules 150

7 Building a Sustainable System **155**
Dealing With AI Fatigue 155
Creating a Culture of Measured Acceleration 158
Clarity Over Tool Sprawl 159
Replacing Effort as Currency 170
Spending Time on What Actually Matters 174
Attach Your Work to Revenue, Not Activity 178
Avoid Becoming the AI Operator 180

8 Spending Time on What Actually Matters 187
AI Parenting Paradox 188
Why Parents Are Getting Left Behind 189
The Lesson They're Already Learning 194
The Signal They're Actually Reading 195
The Difference Between Using a Tool and Modeling One 196
What AI Literacy Actually Looks Like at Home 197
Everyone Starts as a Beginner 200

9 AI Solutions for Employees 201
What Beginners Actually Need 202
Use Cases: 10 Ways to Put Projects and Notebooks to Work 207
Agentic Solutions for Junior and Senior Employees 215

10 Compounding Wins 227
Why Compounding Is the Real Goal 228
The Manager Who Shares Their Wins 229
The Parent Who Makes It a Family Norm 231
The Four-Step Compounding Plan 232

About the Author 237
Index 239

Acknowledgments

This book is dedicated to my son Everett. Everything I do is for you. I am a better person because I am your mom, and that is the greatest gift I have ever been given.

To my husband, thank you for holding down the fort so I never have to choose between being a wife, a mom, and having a career. Your showing up every single day as a stay-at-home dad, homeschooling Everett, and keeping our funny farm running is the reason any of this is possible. The only thing I love more than our life together is the little boy we are raising in it.

Chapter 1

FAQ

Thinking about skipping this chapter? That would be a mistake. These are the questions that separate the people who treat AI as a novelty from the ones who integrate it into their professional lives. If you are not willing to spend a few minutes here, you risk convincing yourself you are ready for AI before you are. Before we get into tools or tactics, I need you to return to an explorer mindset. You should be prepared to doubt information from trusted individuals, embrace not knowing everything, and confront widely accepted ideas that make others uncomfortable.

AI is not just a technological advancement—it is an emotional disruption. It will change how you think about your workday, how you allocate your attention, and what you believe is actually achievable in a given week. That kind of shift can feel overwhelming, so I have gathered the most common questions I hear from professionals who are standing exactly where you are right now. They are curious, a little skeptical, and wondering whether this is all hype.

Why People Are Nervous About Using AI at Work

Q: Will AI replace my job if I automate too much?

A: People exercising judgment, setting direction, and designing work processes are not replaced by AI. What it replaces is the repeated, manual performance of tasks that follow a consistent, predictable sequence. Being limited to that kind of task makes your position insecure. But if your role involves deciding on automation, understanding outcomes, educating users, and aligning output with business aims, it makes you more difficult to replace, not less.

Q: What if I become known only as "the AI person"?

A: This is a legitimate concern, and I have seen it happen. When one person becomes the de facto ChatGPT expert on a team, every conversation starts to go through them, not for strategic reasons, but because they're the only one who knows how to use the interface. That's a ceiling, not a career path. My consistent distinction is between those who operate and those who design. Operators are responsible for running workflows. Architects are responsible for their design, the documentation of their construction, training the surrounding personnel, and aligning the technology with measurable business outcomes. Your influence will reach a ceiling if you continue as an operator. Deliberately pursuing architecture through teaching, documentation, and alignment leads to amplified influence.

Q: Am I too late to start using AI effectively?

A: No. And I say that having trained over 2,500 professionals at this point, many of whom showed up convinced they were already behind. The people who are gaining the most leverage right now are not encyclopedic experts on every new model release. They are consistent experimenters who connect what they are learning to specific outcomes in their actual roles. Momentum matters significantly more than mastery in the early stages. You are only truly late if you keep waiting for the "right" moment to begin.

Q: Do I need to know how to code?

A: Not at all. The key to early advantages, such as gaining weekly time savings and leadership recognition, lies in workflow automation, structured prompting, and a systems-level approach. Coding is useful later on for extensive customization or building your own tools. This is by no means a prerequisite for a meaningful return on investment.

I want to pause here because this particular misconception does more damage than people realize. The overwhelming majority of AI content published today is written for developers, data scientists, and people with engineering backgrounds. Millions of professionals, including those in sales, marketing, operations, customer success, education, and healthcare administration, are excluded from important career and organizational conversations due to this.

This book was written specifically for them. Every framework, every example, every tool recommendation in these pages was deliberately designed to work without writing a single line of code. If you can navigate email, manage a spreadsheet, and use a project management tool, you have everything you need to get started.

Q: What if I experiment and look incompetent?

A: Then start where nobody is watching. Automate an internal process, such as compiling a weekly report, performing a recurring data pull, or rebuilding a monthly template. Measure the before and after. Then share the result with your manager or your team. Competence is not proven by shying away from experiments. It is demonstrated by improving outcomes, and the willingness to try something new is itself a professional signal.

What Risks Should I Actually Be Thinking About?

Q: Is using AI at work dangerous for my job security?

A: It depends entirely on your approach. Here is the pattern I see consistently across organizations: People who automate tasks secretly, without connecting the output to any measurable business impact, create vulnerability for themselves. People who experiment transparently, document what they are building, and tie their work to revenue generation, cost reduction, or operational efficiency build credibility. The risk diminishes substantially when your AI usage is visibly connected to outcomes that leadership already cares about.

Q: How do I use AI safely inside my organization?

A: Start with work that would not cause a problem if the wrong person saw it. Do not put client names, private company plans, or employee information into any AI tool unless your company has said it is okay. If you are not sure what counts as sensitive, ask. That one conversation can save you months of stress. Once you know what is fair game, keep a simple record of what you are using AI for and what results you are getting. That way, if anyone asks what you have been doing, you have the receipts.

Q: What parts of my job could realistically be automated right now?

A: Look for tasks that are repetitive and rules-based, and that predominantly involve compiling, reformatting, or aggregating existing information. If the deliverable is primarily a list, a summary, a structured report, or a data consolidation exercise, it is almost certainly a reasonable automation candidate. The more predictable the inputs and outputs, the stronger the case.

Q: What is the biggest mistake companies make with AI?

A: They rush to automate before anyone agrees on what the basics mean. I have seen this break rollouts at companies of every size. When your marketing team and your sales team both use the word "lead" but one means someone who downloaded a whitepaper and the other means someone ready to buy, automation does not fix that disconnect. It just pushes the wrong people through the pipeline faster.

Before you add speed, make sure everyone is working from the same definitions.

Think of it like this. If you and your partner both agree to "clean the kitchen" but one of you means wiping down the counters and the other means a deep scrub of every appliance, you are going to end up frustrated. Not because anyone did it wrong, but because you never agreed on what "clean" meant in the first place. Now imagine that miscommunication happening across an entire company, at 10 times the speed, because a machine is doing it. That is what happens when you automate before you align on definitions.

Q: Can automation actually hurt productivity?

A: Yes, and it happens more often than most consultants will admit. If you add new tools on top of workflows that were already broken or redundant, you are not making things simpler—you are making the mess move faster. Productivity only improves when everything works together from start to finish. Automating one step in a broken system does not create efficiency; it just speeds up the problem.

What Should I Be Automating?

Q: How do I decide if a task is worth automating?

A: Run it through these four questions: Is the information I need scattered across multiple tools or platforms? Does the task primarily involve searching for or compiling data that already exists somewhere? Could a reasonably competent junior team member complete it if given clear, step-by-step instructions? Does it recur at least once per quarter? If you are answering yes to most of those, you are probably looking at a strong automation candidate.

Q: How do I measure AI ROI without overcomplicating it?

A: Start with time. Measure how long a task takes before automation and how long it takes after. Then multiply the time you saved by how often you do that task, whether that is weekly, monthly, or quarterly. That number is your starting proof that it worked. From there, connect those recovered hours to what you actually did with them. Did you take on more client work? Start a project you had been putting off? Build a relationship that moved the needle? Time is the easiest thing to point to when someone asks if AI is worth it. Once you can show the time saved, tying it back to revenue gets a lot simpler.

Q: How do I know if a tool is worth paying for?

A: If a tool costs $500 a year but saves you $5,000 worth of your time, the math is simple. Too many people get hung up on how many tools they are paying for when the real question is how fast each tool gives you your time back. A tool that costs you money but saves you 10 times that in hours is not an expense. It is one of the smartest investments you can make.

Q: What is the Three-Phase Reduction system?

A: It is a framework I developed for deciding what to do with the work on your plate: Automate what is repetitive and predictable. Delegate what does not genuinely require your personal judgment or expertise. Eliminate what should not exist in the first place. The reports nobody reads. The meetings that could have been emails. The processes that keep happening only because they have always happened. Once you stop doing the things that do not matter, the things that do become obvious.

Q: What new roles are emerging because of AI?

A: New job titles are popping up faster than most people realize, and these are just a few of them:

- AI Product Manager
- AI Workflow Architect
- Automation Strategist
- AI Governance Lead
- Digital Workforce Manager

The list keeps growing. What all of these roles have in common is that the hands-on, repetitive work is disappearing and the thinking work is taking its place. Designing how systems run. Making sure the output is accurate. Connecting the dots between departments. The people getting hired for these jobs are not always the most technical. They are the ones who can look at what AI does and figure out how it solves a real problem for the business.

How Do I Prevent AI From Consuming My Life?

Q: If AI makes me faster, won't expectations just increase?

A: Almost certainly, unless you decide ahead of time that it will not. When AI saves you time, that time does not just sit there waiting for you. It gets filled. More meetings. More messages. More people asking for "just one quick thing." Before you automate anything significant, decide where that saved time is going. If you do not protect it, someone else will claim it. And you will end up working just as hard, producing more than before, with nothing to show for it personally.

Q: How do I protect strategic thinking time?

A: Automate the repetitive work first. That is what creates the breathing room. Then block off time for deep, focused thinking and treat those blocks like a meeting with your CEO. Nobody cancels those. Stop making yourself available every second of the day just because you can respond. Close Slack. Close your email. The fact that you are reachable does not mean you should always be reached. How visible you are at work should be something you choose, not something that happens because you never log off.

Q: What should I do with the time AI saves me?

A: Be intentional about where it goes. The best use of saved time is usually one of four things: (a) learning something new that makes you more valuable over time; (b) building relationships with people who can open doors for you; (c) creating things you can reuse, like templates, processes, or frameworks; or (d) finally working on the big ideas that keep getting buried under your daily to-do list. If your saved time just turns into more meetings and more busywork, nothing has actually changed—you have just moved the pile from one side of your desk to the other.

Q: How do I avoid AI fatigue and cognitive overload?

A: Give yourself a set time to try new tools and stick to it. Do not let every shiny new app that launches steal your afternoon. Before you add any tool to your workflow, know exactly what problem it is solving and how you will measure whether it actually works. If it does not save you real time within a few weeks, get rid of it. The people who burn out on AI are almost always the ones who keep downloading new tools and mistaking that for making progress.

Q: How do I ensure I am building leverage, not just speed?

A: Move upstream. Stop focusing exclusively on how fast you can execute tasks and start focusing on decision quality, system architecture, and cross-functional alignment. Speed is becoming commoditized, so everyone with access to these tools can move faster. Exercising good judgment, knowing how to build systems that work across teams, and being able to spot what should never have been built in the first place are skills that are rare—and rare is where your value lives.

You now have straightforward answers to the questions that almost everyone asks when they first think about bringing AI into their work and their life. But here is the truth that nobody talks about: No one is an expert in AI because the tools change every single day. I have watched people spend hundreds of hours tinkering with settings and never get anywhere, and I have watched others completely change how they work in a matter of weeks. The difference between those two groups is not talent or luck. It is knowing what problem you are trying to solve before you ever open a tool.

AI can eat your time just as easily as it can save it. I can hand you the blueprint, but only you can make the decision to stop scrolling through what everyone else is saying about these tools and actually use them to fix something real in your own work.

Nobody handed me an AI playbook. I built mine through trial and error, through moments where I was genuinely excited and stretches where I wanted to throw my laptop across the room. The turning point for me was when I stopped treating AI like something fun to experiment with and started asking myself how it could actually help me hit the goals I already had.

When everyone on your team is using the same language, repetitive work is handled automatically, and your brainpower is protected for the decisions that actually matter, that is when speed turns into something that lasts instead of just creating more noise. The rest of this book is going to show you exactly how to make that happen.

But this did not come out of nowhere for me. It came from a specific moment in my life that forced me to completely rethink what was possible and how I wanted my work to look. That is the story I am going to tell you next, so you can see how to create your own turning point starting right now.

Chapter 2

Assess Your Current Workflow

You were told the rules early. Work harder than everyone else. Stay later. Respond faster. If you outwork the room, you will always be safe.

Nobody questioned it. Nobody wrote it down. And nobody told you what it was actually costing you.

This book does.

The True Cost

My mentors made winning at work sound simple. Be the hardest worker in the room. Stay later than everyone else. Respond faster than anyone expects. If you can outwork the people around you, you will always be safe.

Nobody ever wrote that rule down, but everything in the culture reinforced it. Supervisors praised the people who stayed up late. Colleagues trusted the ones who responded instantly. Being busy looked like being important, and exhaustion looked like commitment.

So that became my identity. When projects failed, my hand went up. When someone needed coverage, my calendar absorbed it. Late-night calls, urgent client emails, weekends that disappeared into work that felt critical in the moment but barely mattered a month later. Holidays were spent catching up. Hospital rooms became makeshift offices. Personal plans got pushed aside because being needed felt the same as being valuable.

Over time, slowing down stopped feeling like a choice and started feeling like a threat. Even a small step back felt like losing ground that could never be recovered.

Responsiveness became the way relevance was measured. A fast reply meant you mattered. Constant availability meant you were useful. The speed of the answer became more important than the quality of the thinking behind it.

Rest never felt like rest. It came with a low hum of guilt, like borrowed time that would need to be repaid later. Even away from the desk, part of my brain stayed locked on what might be falling through the cracks. Explaining how hard the work was came easily. Explaining what all that effort actually moved forward was a different conversation entirely.

At some point, the question of whether this was healthy just stopped coming up. This was just how work was. Meaningful work probably always felt this heavy. The knot in your stomach that never went away was just what ambition felt like. Being tired all the time was simply part of the deal. Then one day, in a meeting that lasted less than 10 minutes, everything I believed about work fell apart.

"We do not offer maternity leave."

The words hung there for a second, like they needed time to register. Then they dropped hard, with no apology, no explanation, and no pause to let the meaning sink in. Before I could even respond they moved on. "Would you like to hear about our daycare options?"

That was it. No acknowledgment of the years I had given them, no recognition of the moment I was in, no sign that they saw me as anything more than a resource to be managed. I sat through their daycare pitch, nodded at the right moments, and kept my voice polite, but inside I was boiling.

Walking out of that meeting, something had shifted and there was no pretending otherwise. All the loyalty, the late nights, the energy poured into that company without hesitation did not make me valuable to them. It made me predictable, and predictable was not an asset. It was a liability they could count on.

My husband had just been laid off, so quitting was not on the table. Instead, the instinct was to do what most people do when they feel trapped. Work harder. Become so essential that they could never let go. That plan backfired almost immediately.

My calendar had turned into a war zone, with meetings packed from morning to night, Slack messages firing at all hours, and an inbox that never stopped filling with requests that all felt urgent to someone. Everyone leaned on me to fix their problems, but the feeling that came with it was not one of being valued. It was one of being used. Nightmares about unexpected Teams calls started creeping in, and just the sight of that red notification dot on Slack was enough to make my chest tighten. The last time a task had been finished start to finish without a single interruption was a memory too far back to even reach.

By that point, the overwhelm had become so constant and so deep that putting it into words felt almost impossible. So one afternoon, almost out of pure desperation, an hour got blocked on the calendar with no calls, no messages, and no interruptions. Just a blinking cursor and the chance to think without being pulled in 10 different directions at once.

Even that small act felt uncomfortable. What would it look like to others if the calendar showed an hour of blocked time with no explanation? What would the response be if someone asked why that time was unavailable? There was a real and genuine fear that taking one hour to sit and think would be seen by everyone else as not actually working.

That single hour changed everything. For the first time, it became clear that there was no real sense of how long the actual work took each day. Every morning ran straight into every afternoon, bouncing from one thing to the next, treating everyone else's emergencies like they were my own, without ever stopping to ask how much of that time was spent on work that actually mattered.

The decision was to start tracking all of it, with nothing fancy and no overthinking. A free Chrome extension called Toggl was installed, and it recorded everything throughout the day. Starting and stopping a timer, sorting work into categories, and tagging how each task felt was all it took. Everything got tracked, down to the minute and the gut reaction that came with it.

What came back was staggering. Eight hours a week answering and organizing emails. Six hours sitting in meetings that could have been handled in a quick message. Five hours updating spreadsheets by hand. Four hours writing reports that already existed somewhere else in a different format. When it was all added up, 23 hours every single week were going toward work that did not require any judgment, creativity, or experience to complete.

Think about what that actually costs. If you earn $70,000 a year, 23 hours of low value work per week means roughly $46,000 of your salary is being spent on tasks that do not need you. At $95,000, that number jumps to $62,000. At $140,000, it climbs to $91,000. Now multiply that across a team of 10 people. That is not a productivity gap. That is a six-figure leak that nobody budgeted for and nobody is measuring. It is not a time management problem. It is a business problem hiding inside your calendar.

The part that was truly unsettling had nothing to do with how busy things were. It was realizing there was no clear picture of what a good day was even supposed to look like. Recognizing exhaustion was easy because it showed up every single day. Recognizing when the work was actually effective, when the hours spent genuinely moved something forward, was a completely different story and one that did not have an obvious answer.

That gap between being active and being effective is where most careers quietly stall out. And the worst part is that most people never even notice it happening because the busyness feels like proof that they are doing enough. The tools filling up your day are not the real problem. The real problem is that nobody has ever sat you down and asked you to define what your judgment, your thinking, and your experience are actually worth in hours and dollars. As more of the routine work becomes something a machine can handle, that question stops being the kind of thing you wonder about in the shower and starts being the thing that determines what you earn and whether your role survives the next round of changes.

A few days later, something small happened that ended up changing everything. Lunch was being made, and a podcast was playing in the background when the host casually mentioned a founder who had built an AI tool designed specifically for marketers—not for engineers or developers or anyone with a computer science degree, but for people who did the work that filled up my days. That one word landed differently than anything else had in months, and it would not stop pulling at the back of my mind. For the first time in a very long time, the feeling sitting in my chest was not exhaustion or frustration or the dread of another overloaded week. It was curiosity, real and electric, the kind that makes you forget what you were doing and start Googling before the podcast episode even finishes. That curiosity was about to change the entire direction of my career.

My first instinct was to tune it out entirely. Marketers do not need more tools. What we need is fewer tabs open and fewer platforms pulling us in different directions. The founder went on to talk about how he had spent years as a project manager across multiple companies, overseeing their marketing departments and watching the same problems repeat themselves everywhere he went. Endless busywork that never seemed to shrink. Repetitive tasks that ate through the day before any real thinking could happen. Hours and hours lost to email that should have been spent on actual strategy.

Then he explained how his AI tool could learn a company's brand voice and tone, apply custom rules, and rewrite an entire inbox in minutes. The way he described it, this tool sounded like the marketing assistant every team has always wished they had but could never afford. Faster, cheaper, and ready to go at any hour of the day. That part made me stop what I was doing. Even if half of it was exaggerated, the other half was worth seeing with my own eyes.

The plan was to give it 30 minutes, just long enough to prove it was overhyped and move on with my day. The subject lines from my inbox got copied over, more than 80 emails worth, along with one simple instruction. Organize these by urgency. One minute later, a clean and perfectly organized list sat on the screen. Then the tool asked if it should draft the replies.

Eight hours of work had just collapsed into 60 seconds, and the feeling that followed was not excitement. My stomach dropped. Not because the tool was impressive, although it was, but because of what it meant. Years had been spent getting fast, accurate, and dependable, believing that consistency was the edge that made my work valuable. And now a tool had done the same thing in a fraction of the time without making a single mistake. It was a strange and uncomfortable mix of awe and genuine unease.

For a long moment, the cursor just hovered between closing the tab and clicking deeper. It was the same feeling that hits when you first realize something you have spent years perfecting could be done without you. Unsettling and a little humbling, but completely impossible to ignore.

Identifying Inefficiencies in Your Workday

This is the moment where most people stop, not because the tool does not work, but because it works too well and threatens the entire identity that was carefully built around being the person who is always needed and always available.

All the productivity advice in the world does not help with what comes next. Better time management, sharper focus, more discipline—none of that matters when you are staring at a screen that just did eight hours of your work in under a minute. The only question left is one that no productivity tip has ever tried to answer. If the work that filled my days can vanish that fast, then what exactly am I bringing to the table that a machine cannot?

That question followed me around for days, long after the tab was closed and the tool was forgotten. The choice it left behind was simple but deeply uncomfortable: go back to filling the day with the same busywork and pretend that moment never happened, or keep pulling the thread and risk finding out that some of the work that felt so important and so worth defending was never really worth protecting at all. You already know which direction I chose, or this book would not exist.

When the first serious time audit happened, the obvious offenders were exactly what you would expect. Endless meetings that accomplished nothing, reports that nobody read, and fire drills disguised as urgent projects that turned out to be anything but. They were all there taking their predictable toll on the week, but they turned out not to be the biggest problem by a long shot.

The real issue was not how much effort was going in but how little impact was coming out. All of that activity kept things moving on the surface, but it moved nothing forward in any meaningful way. The calendar looked full, the task list looked productive, and the actual results looked exactly the same as they had the month before.

The biggest drain on my time turned out to be the small things that barely even registered as work because they always showed up wearing the costume of someone else's emergency. Things like replying to "Thanks!" emails that never needed a response in the first place, or manually entering the same sales data into two completely separate systems because nobody had ever bothered to connect them, or quietly cleaning up someone else's repeated mistakes because fixing it in the moment always felt faster than sitting down and having the awkward conversation about why it kept happening.

Each of these tiny tasks took less than 5 minutes, and 5 minutes feels so completely harmless that it never occurs to anyone to push back on it. It is too short to justify changing a process over and too small to bother optimizing in any formal way. The thought is always the same, that it will just take a second, and then it is done and forgotten about until the same thing shows up again tomorrow morning.

The math behind those harmless minutes is where it starts to get brutal. A 5-minute task done five times a day adds up to 25 minutes, which turns into 125 minutes every single week, which becomes over 108 hours across a full year. That is for just one small recurring task. Stretched across 12 months, that is nearly two full weeks of vacation quietly lost to something that does not produce a single meaningful result that anyone would notice or remember.

Now imagine there are 10 of those micro-tasks scattered across every single day, and for most people the real number is far higher than 10. A quick Slack reply that takes 30 seconds, a form that needs to be filled out before lunch, a small chunk of data that has to be copied from one platform to another because nobody ever took the time to set up the integration between them. When all of those moments are added together over the course of a year, what you are looking at is months of your working life quietly given away one seemingly harmless moment at a time. The truly unsettling part is that it never once feels like a choice because each individual moment is so small and so quick that it does not seem worth questioning or pushing back on.

It is not just the minutes that disappear when this happens, though. It is the focus, which in many ways ends up being even more expensive than the time itself. Every single time deep, concentrated work gets interrupted to handle one of those small tasks, the brain has to completely reset and find its way back to wherever it left off before the interruption pulled it away. That recovery time, the mental effort of shifting gears and rebuilding the full context of what you were thinking about and where you were headed with it, almost always takes significantly longer than the interruption that caused it. A 5-minute task does not actually cost 5 minutes. It costs 5 minutes plus the 15 or 20 minutes it takes to get back into the flow of the original work, which means the true cost of all those constant micro-interruptions stacked on top of each other throughout the day is something most people have never sat down to calculate and would be genuinely alarmed to see if they did.

The work was entirely reactive and came from every direction without any warning, which meant there was never a natural stopping point to any of it. It regenerated faster than it could ever be cleared, like trying to empty a bathtub while the faucet is still running full blast, where the only reward for finally getting through one pile was discovering another pile sitting right behind it that had built up while you were busy with the first one.

Once all of this was laid out in real numbers that could not be argued with or explained away, the same set of questions started running through my mind every single time something new landed on my plate. Once the math became impossible to ignore, staying in denial about what was really happening got harder and harder with every passing week. Hours and weeks and months of time and energy were being burned on tasks that were quietly stealing the ability to take a real vacation without checking email, to say no to things without that familiar wave of guilt, or to actually spend energy on the projects and relationships that led somewhere worth going instead of just treading water in the same spot day after day.

At a certain point, inefficiency stops being an abstract concept that other people write about in business books and talk about at seminars. It starts to feel deeply and uncomfortably personal. It shows up as burnout long before anyone around you uses that word to describe what they are watching happen to you. It shows up as the quiet, nagging sense that you are always behind no matter how many hours you put in or how early you drag yourself out of bed to get a head start on the day. It shows up as the creeping doubt that maybe the problem was never the workload at all, but something fundamental about the way the work itself has always been structured that nobody has ever stopped long enough to look at, let alone question.

What Tasks Waste the Most Time at Work

Most managers will tell you what your priorities are. They rarely show you how to measure whether you are hitting them. That gap is where things start to get messy and where busywork sneaks in without anyone noticing.

Ask the follow-up yourself: "What does a successful outcome look like for each of these?" The moment you ask that question, priorities stop being vague and start turning into outcomes.

Once outcomes are clear, you finally have something most people never get: a way to tell which work actually deserves your time. You have a filter, and that filter is what makes AI genuinely helpful.

Start by creating three categories, one for each priority or outcome you identified with your manager. For example:

- Launch Messaging
- Sales Support
- Issue Reduction

If you use color coding, I strongly recommend a red, yellow, green system:

- Red: Highest impact, most time sensitive
- Yellow: Important but flexible
- Green: Helpful, but not critical

From there, use your AI assistant to help organize your work around those outcomes. If your company runs on Microsoft tools like Outlook and Microsoft 365, Copilot can help sort and categorize your emails and calendar, so you can see where your time is going. If your company uses Google Workspace instead, Gemini can do the same thing within Gmail and Google Calendar. Either way, both tools can help you line up how you spend your time and who you communicate with against the priorities that actually matter most to your role and your goals.

Create inbox labels that match your outcomes:

- Launch Messaging
- Sales Support
- Issue Reduction

Use either Copilot or Gemini to scan your inbox and suggest how to organize it.

You can prompt it directly with: "These are my three work priorities right now: Launch Messaging, Sales Support, and Issue

Reduction. Can you scan my inbox and suggest labels for emails based on which priority they support?"

For longer emails, ask either Copilot or Gemini to summarize and highlight alignment.

You can ask it something as simple as "Summarize this thread and tell me which of my priorities it supports, if any." Instead of treating every message in your inbox like it carries the same weight, you start to see which conversations are tied to real outcomes and which ones are just noise that happens to be loud enough to demand your attention.

Once your inbox is categorized, open your calendar. The same outcome categories you created for email should live here too. As you look through your upcoming week, right-click on each meeting and assign it to the priority it supports. This forces a quiet but powerful question: What is this meeting actually for? When every meeting must belong to an outcome, patterns surface quickly. Some meetings clearly earn their place. Others feel suddenly optional. A few stand out as confusing because no one can quite explain what success looks like.

At the end of the week, review your calendar honestly. Look at how your time was spent, not how you hoped it would be spent. Which categories dominated your schedule? Which priorities barely showed up at all? Were there meetings that are never really connected to a clear outcome? This is where small boundaries start to matter.

If you come across an email or meeting that does not genuinely require your involvement, there is no need to write a paragraph explaining why you are stepping back. A clear and respectful response is almost always enough. Something along the lines of "My top three priorities this week are X, Y, and Z, and I will follow up asynchronously where needed." That kind of response accomplishes two things at once. It communicates your focus in a professional way that nobody can argue with, and it shifts the entire conversation away from whether you are available and toward what you are working to accomplish, which is where your real value has always been.

Instead of leaving my inbox open all day and responding to things as they come in, I block specific time on my calendar just for email. Three times a day, no more than 20 minutes each, at 8 a.m., 1 p.m., and 4 p.m. Those blocks are treated like real meetings that cannot be moved or talked over. During those windows, every email gets a full and thoughtful response. Outside of them, the inbox stays closed and the focus stays on the work that actually needs my brain.

When an email comes in that requires thought or emotional energy, I do not try to squeeze it in. I use the desktop version of my Outlook email and drag the message directly onto my calendar. It creates a meeting block between me and that email. All the context, attachments, and history live right there. When the time comes to sit down and deal with it, everything needed is already right there instead of having to dig back through the thread trying to remember what mattered and what the next step was supposed to be.

What took a long time to realize was that the anxiety around stepping away from work had nothing to do with motivation or discipline. It was rooted in fear, the kind that convinces you that forgetting one important thing or missing one follow-up or looking away for even a moment will cause the whole thing to come crashing down. Carrying all of that around invisibly was exhausting in a way that never showed up on a to-do list, and it turns out that most of it never needed to live inside my head in the first place.

Whether your company runs on Google or Microsoft, tools like Gemini and Copilot can hold all of that context for you so your brain does not have to. At the end of every day, usually around 4:30, I started giving my AI tool one simple instruction before wrapping up:

Prompt: "Summarize any emails I have not responded to that relate to my top priorities, and any meeting follow-ups I have not completed that are tagged as pending. Aggregate this into a short, podcast style set of notes."

Sometimes that summary played through my headphones on the drive home, and other times it played in the background while packing up my desk for the night. Either way, hearing everything laid out clearly in one place gave my brain permission to let go of the day instead of running through a mental checklist on repeat all evening. Nothing was forgotten and nothing was slipping through the cracks because it was all captured in one place.

On days when surfacing all of that before leaving felt like too much, the prompt got adjusted and scheduled to send the summary first thing the next morning at 7:30 instead. That way, the moment the workday started, there was already a clear picture of exactly where to pick up and what needed attention first without having to spend the first hour of the morning trying to piece it all back together.

Mapping Your Weekly Workflow

When you look at your day through outcomes instead of tasks, it becomes clear that not all work deserves the same human attention. Some steps require judgment and relationships. Others exist only because no one has questioned them. Start by breaking down your processes step by step to see where work loops, regenerates, and consumes time without creating value.

The easiest way to think about it is through an outcome you already understand. Getting to work by 7:50 a.m. That is the outcome. It is the thing you are trying to achieve.

Your workflow is the path that gets you there. It includes everything that has to happen along the way. Remember to grab your lunch from the fridge. Leaving the house at 7:30 for a 20-minute commute. Making sure your gas tank is full. Inside that workflow are individual processes. Packing your lunch. Driving to work. Filling up the car. Each of those processes can be handled efficiently or inefficiently, and the choices compound.

If you pack your lunch in the morning, it eats into the time you need to leave on schedule. If you forget to get gas the night before, you add an unexpected stop and extra stress to the morning. None of these things change the outcome you want. They just make the workflow heavier. Over time, that weight is what makes success feel harder to reach, even when nothing about the goal itself has changed.

This is why efficiency has to be examined at the process level—not to optimize everything but to remove the friction that quietly makes success feel out of reach. Once you can see how processes stack inside a workflow, you can decide which ones deserve your attention and which ones should be simplified, delegated, or automated.

Capturing your processes does not have to be complicated. In practice, there are only two scenarios:

- In the first, the process is already written down and the documentation actually reflects how the work is done today. If that is true, you are in great shape. Use that document as your starting point.
- In the second, which is far more common, there is no real standard operating procedure (SOP) or the one that exists no longer matches reality. The work has drifted. Shortcuts have been added. Context lives in your head. In that case, the fastest and most accurate way to capture the process is to record yourself completing the work. This is the approach I use.

Create a meeting with yourself. When you join, turn on recording and transcription. Share your screen and simply do the work as you normally would. As you go, narrate what you are doing and why.

Do not worry about being polished. Stumble if you need to. Pause. Backtrack. The goal is not perfection. The goal is truth. You are creating a record of how the work actually happens, not how it was supposed to happen.

Once the recording ends, take the transcript and upload it into your AI tool of choice. I personally use Copilot or Gemini, and ChatGPT works just as well if your company allows it. Any modern model can handle this. Prompt it with something simple like: "Organize this transcript by process name, tools used, steps taken in each tool, and the purpose of each step. Return the full process in that format."

In just a few minutes, you will have created a usable SOP that did not exist before. If your team has never had documentation for this process, this immediately cuts down on the amount of time a real person has to spend training every new hire who walks through the door. If documentation already existed somewhere, you now have a version that reflects how the work is actually being done today instead of how someone imagined it was being done when they wrote the original version three years ago.

What matters even more is that you now have something you can examine and pick apart. You can see where steps are being repeated unnecessarily, where tools overlap with each other in ways nobody planned, and where effort is being wasted on things that do not contribute to the final result. That kind of visibility makes it so much easier to improve the process before handing it off to another person or turning it over to automation.

If the process turns out to be a strong candidate for automation down the road, this documentation becomes the blueprint for making that happen. There is no more guessing about how the work runs day to day because it has all been captured exactly as it exists right now, which means any tool that gets introduced later can be measured against whether it genuinely speeds things up or just adds another layer of complexity on top of what was already there.

At this stage, there are always a few well-meaning people who want to skip ahead and ask AI to do the work for them. It is understandable. The tools feel powerful, and it is tempting to jump straight to automation. That shortcut almost always backfires.

Even if you have a process written down, it does not automatically mean it is a good one. Many teams are still following documentation created years ago by someone who no longer works at the company. Over time, people adapt, patch, and work around that process, but the document never gets updated. Humans are surprisingly inefficient. That is not a flaw. It is just how work evolves—which means training AI to take over parts of your job requires first validating that the process itself still makes sense.

Before I automate anything, I take the SOP generated from my recording and run it back through the AI with a different set of prompts. Not to execute the work, but to interrogate it. I prompt questions like:

- Where are the manual or repetitive steps in this process that could realistically be automated using this tool?
- Which steps could be removed, combined, or delegated without changing the outcome?
- How would a high-performing team run this process differently to get the same results with less effort?

What I am looking for is not the entire process to disappear—I am looking for pressure points. Every process breaks down into a few smaller processes. Intake. Organization. Decision-making. Follow-up. Some of those steps require judgment. Some require context. Others are simply rules being applied over and over again. Those rule-based steps are where you start.

Let's make this real with a process almost everyone recognizes. Onboarding a new request. On the surface, it feels like one process.

A request comes in, you get to work, and eventually something gets delivered. But when AI actually broke that process down, it turned out to be several smaller processes stitched together.

First came intake, which meant understanding what was being asked and why it was being asked in the first place. Then came clarification, filling in the missing context and making sure everyone was aligned on what the expectations actually were. After that came organization, translating the request into specific tasks, realistic timelines, and the right tools to get it done. Finally there was follow-up, making sure nothing fell through the cracks between the moment the work started and the moment it was delivered.

Every process has steps that follow clear rules, save meaningful time, and practically beg to be automated because the risk is low and the return is high. Other steps carry real risk with very little payoff, and those are better left in human hands, at least for now. Most steps fall somewhere in between those two extremes. What keeps people from over automating is taking one familiar process, breaking it down into its individual parts, and evaluating each step on its own merits instead of trying to automate the whole thing at once. That is what makes the difference between automating with intention and automating out of impulse.

Intake and organization land squarely in the low-risk, high-return category because they follow consistent rules every single time. Neither one requires judgment or interpretation; they simply take information that already exists and turn it into something structured and usable. Clarification is a completely different story and sits much higher on the risk side. It depends on context, nuance, and real conversation between actual people, which means automating it too early tends to create more confusion than speed. Follow-up falls somewhere in between those two. It offers strong returns when done well, but tone and timing still matter enough that it benefits from having clear guardrails in place before handing it over to full automation.

The best place to start is organizing your intake. One simple automation, maintained over two to three weeks, can unlock hours of time and prevent chaos from creeping in. All you need is a project management tool. This method works with nearly every major platform—Jira, Asana, Monday, and most other task tools on the market.

Start by exporting your existing tasks into a CSV file. Then upload that file into your AI assistant and ask it to create a task intake template. The AI can analyze your data and return a structured template with field names and dropdown options that reflect the types of work you regularly handle. This gives you a standardized form that can be prefilled by anyone assigning you a task.

If you use a tool like Monday, Asana, or Jira, you already have more enforcement power than you think. All three platforms allow you to bake structure directly into the work itself. You can require specific fields before a task or request is created. You can prevent work from moving forward if key information is missing. You can trigger automatic comments, status changes, or rerouting when someone skips a step. In other words, the system can enforce the rules for you.

Efficiency compounds when you start small and stay consistent. One automation, done well and adopted fully, creates the space for the next. Give this first change at least two weeks to settle.

Here is your move. Pick one process you completed this week. Create a meeting with yourself, share your screen, hit Record, and do the work out loud. When you are done, upload the transcript and use the prompt from this chapter. You will have a usable SOP in minutes. Do this before the end of the week. The recording does not need to be polished; it needs to be real.

If improvement were purely technical, most teams would already be faster. What slows things down is fear of getting it wrong. Fear of being judged after the fact. Fear of invisible rules. Until that fear is addressed, no amount of automation will scale. That is why the next chapter focuses on psychological safety.

Which Work Activities Should Never Be Automated

Most workplaces say they want innovation, but what they reward is predictability. Do the work the way it has already been approved. Do not break anything. Do not create risk. That is why the only experiments that survive approval are the ones that feel boring. They are small enough to ignore, constrained enough to control, and reversible enough that no one has to defend them.

That is the purpose of the box. It creates a narrow space where work can be examined without triggering fear. Think of the box as a boundary around work, not a tool.

Inside the box is where all the preparation happens. Drafting, summarizing, organizing, classifying, and cutting through noise all live here, and the reason this space is safe for automation is that nothing final happens inside it. Work can be wrong and it does not matter because there is always a chance to catch it and fix it before anyone else ever sees it.

Outside the box is where commitment lives. Sending, publishing, approving, making decisions, and changing records are all actions that create real impact the moment they happen and cannot be quietly undone after the fact. The rule that separates the two is simple. Automation can operate as freely as it wants inside the box, where mistakes are safe, observable, and easy to correct. It stops at the edge of the box, right where real responsibility and real consequences begin.

This is the principle that separates teams who use AI well from teams who use it recklessly. Automation does not replace judgment. It makes judgment sharper and more effective, but only when it is applied to the right part of the process. When the preparation, the organization, the pattern recognition, and the noise reduction are all handled before a human being ever has to make a call, that person gets something they almost never have in most workplaces: a clear signal at the exact moment it matters most. The goal is never to pull people out of the process entirely—the goal is to strip away everything that was preventing them from thinking clearly while they were inside it.

There is another boundary that operates alongside the box, and this one is non-negotiable. Not every piece of data belongs in every tool, no matter how convenient it might be to put it there. Before connecting a system or uploading a file, three questions need to be answered honestly.

The first question to ask is whether the tool you are using is approved by your company to handle business data. If your organization has not given the green light on a specific AI tool, do not paste customer names, deal sizes, internal strategy, or employee details into it. Saving a few minutes is never worth the risk of putting sensitive information somewhere it was never meant to go.

The second question is whether the data you are working with is protected by any laws or industry rules. Things like health records, financial data, and personal information often fall under regulations like the General Data Protection Regulation (GDPR), the Health Insurance Portability and Accountability Act (HIPAA), or System and Organization Controls 2 (SOC 2), and those rules require very specific tools that meet very specific standards. Running patient data through a tool that has not been approved for that kind of information is not a time-saver—it is a problem waiting to happen at the worst possible time.

The third question is the easiest one to ask and often the hardest one to hear the answer to. If this data got out tomorrow, what would happen? If the answer is lawsuits, fines, lost customer trust, or giving a competitor information they should never have, then that data should not touch an automation until someone responsible for security and compliance has reviewed it and said yes.

This is not about making AI harder to adopt or putting up roadblocks for the sake of caution. It is about making sure that the time you save does not come with a hidden cost you cannot take back once the damage is done. Start with data that would not cause a problem if something went wrong, prove that the workflow does what it is supposed to do, and only move toward more sensitive information after the right people in your organization have looked at how it all works and given their approval.

A downloadable data sensitivity checklist for evaluating which workflows are safe to automate and which ones require compliance review first is available at `http://myaiworkweek.com/datasafety`.

Some parts of your job carry too much weight to ever be fully handed off to a machine, no matter how smart that machine gets. These are the parts that define who is trusted, who is accountable, and whose judgment the organization relies on when it matters most. Automating them does not make things run smoother. It makes it impossible to figure out who is responsible when something goes wrong. Any decision that locks the company into a direction, speaks to the outside world on behalf of the business, or puts a stamp on something as true and accurate needs a real person behind it. Not because AI cannot draft it or organize it or prepare it, because it absolutely can, but because someone still has to own the final call and be able to look another person in the eye and explain why that choice was made.

Work that changes records, sends messages, or finalizes outcomes should stay out of automation until accountability is explicit. Here is what this looks like when it goes wrong. A mid-sized SaaS company automated their renewal process end to end. The system generated contracts, applied pricing, and sent them to customers without human review. For three months it worked. Then a pricing rule misfired and 340 accounts received contracts with rates 18 percent below what had been approved. By the time someone noticed, 87 of those contracts had been signed. Legal spent four months unwinding the damage. The company absorbed over $200,000 in revenue it could not recover. The automation was not the problem. The missing approval gate was. There was no human checkpoint between the system generating the contract and the system sending it. The box had no edge. When you hear someone say automation increases risk, this is what they mean. Not that the technology fails. That accountability was never designed into the workflow. Every automation that touches pricing, contracts, customer communication, or compliance requires an explicit approval step before anything leaves the building. If you cannot point to the person who reviewed it, the system is not ready.

Boundaries reduce fear faster than encouragement ever will. When employees know what will not be automated, they do not have to guess where the risk lives. That is what makes exploration possible without asking anyone to gamble their credibility. Not every task deserves automation, and not every inefficiency is a problem worth solving. The next chapter is about deciding where AI actually belongs and where it does not.

Before you turn this page, do one thing. Download Toggl or open whatever timer you have on your phone. Set it for your next work block and label it honestly. You are not optimizing yet. You are just watching. Give yourself one full workday of tracking before you move on. Start within 48 hours. If you want the exact tracking template I used, it is at `http://myaiworkweek.com/timeaudit`.

Chapter 3

Identifying Automation Opportunities

When I first started automating my workflow, I made the same mistake almost everyone makes. I chased the big, flashy wins first. I thought the bigger the automation, the bigger the payoff. I wanted the kind of thing I could show off in a meeting and have people say, "Wow, how did you do that?" Those game-changing projects eventually paid off. But they also took weeks of setup, testing, and tweaking. Some stalled halfway because urgent work pulled me in another direction. More than once, I looked at an unfinished automation and realized it had been sitting untouched for months.

Automation is not about starting with the biggest thing you can find or picking off the easiest task just to check a box. It is about balance. You need wins that show up fast enough to prove to yourself and sometimes to your team that this actually works, and you need longer-term projects that have the potential to fundamentally change how you operate day to day. Without those quick wins, the motivation to keep going fizzles out before you ever get to the good stuff. Without the bigger projects that take more time and thought, you will never move past surface-level improvements that look nice but do not really change anything.

I started thinking of it like building a portfolio. Quick wins were the cash flow—they paid off immediately, kept me moving, and built trust in the process. Game changers were the long-term investments—slower to mature but capable of delivering exponential returns. Quick wins are the low-hanging fruit—automations you can set up in under an hour that save measurable time right away. They're usually simple, repetitive tasks that happen daily or weekly.

Game changers are the automations that fundamentally reshape how you work. They often take days or weeks to implement, but once they're live, the impact is so big you can't imagine going back. Anything that takes less than 2 hours to set up and saves more than 10 hours a year is a quick win. Anything that takes morc than a week to set up but saves over 100 hours a year or creates a measurable business impact is a game changer. Then create a rotation. Implement one quick win, then one game changer, then another quick win. This keeps your momentum while building toward long-term impact.

Repetitive Tasks AI Can Automate at Work

If a task is boring, drains your energy, or keeps pulling you away from the work you were hired to do, there is a good chance a machine can handle it for you. Most people are not stuck because they are out of ideas or do not know what needs to happen next. They are stuck because so much of their day gets swallowed up by things that are not the real work. Sending updates. Chasing people down. Sitting in meetings about meetings. Explaining the same thing for the third time that week. By the time all of that is done, the actual work barely gets touched.

Here are four quick wins in the order I recommend tackling them, and every single one of them delivers real, noticeable results fast. What makes these so great is that if your company already uses Google Workspace or Microsoft Copilot with the AI features turned on, you can start doing them today. No new software. No special permissions. No waiting on IT. They all run on the tools you are already using every day, like email, calendar, documents, meetings, and task managers.

Async Team Updates Without Rewriting Your Own Brain

Think about how many hours you have spent tracking down updates that could have been pulled automatically from work that already happened. Or sitting through a weekly meeting where nobody bothered to send an agenda. Or hopping on a "quick check-in" call with someone who shows up with nothing prepared and asks the same questions that could have been answered in a two-line email. None of that is leadership. It is busywork dressed up as teamwork, and every single one of those moments is something a machine could handle better and faster than any human ever will.

How to Set This Up

Start by choosing your data sources, which are the systems that already track what you are working on every day. These should include your calendar along with any meeting transcripts, your task or project management tools like Asana, and whatever collaboration platforms your team uses like Teams channels, email threads, or Slack.

Next, set clear rules for what the AI should and should not do. You are not asking it to be creative or make guesses. You are asking it to be disciplined and stick to the facts.

Prompt: "Use only data I already have access to. Look at the past five business days of emails, meetings, and Asana tasks or boards where my name appears as an owner, participant, assignee, or mention. Only include items that contain the phrases product launch, sales support for MVP launch, or launch messaging. Do not include any other work."

After that, define exactly what you want the output to look like. This is not a performance review or a chance for the AI to impress anyone. It is a factual progress report, and the AI needs to know the exact structure you expect.

Prompt: "Based only on the items identified above, generate a concise weekly update written in plain language. Organize the summary into three sections: what progressed, what is blocked or at risk, and what is next. Focus on outcomes and movement, not activity."

Finally, lock down the tone so the AI keeps things neutral and honest without trying to make the work sound better or more complete than it actually is.

Prompt: "Do not invent tasks, goals, timelines, or outcomes. Do not reword the work to sound more positive or more complete than it is. Only summarize what is explicitly present in the emails, meetings, and Asana items. If information is missing or unclear, state that directly instead of filling in gaps."

For this whole system to work, every person involved needs to leave a visible trail in the tools they are already using every day. That means a few things need to become habit.

Transcribe your meetings by using tools like Teams, Zoom, or Otter to automatically record and transcribe every call. If a conversation is not recorded somewhere, it basically did not happen as far as the AI is concerned.

Keep your tasks up to date. You do not have to manage the entire board, but you do need to mark what has been started, what is done, and what is stuck or blocked.

Use the right keywords in your notes. If your weekly update needs to show progress on the "product launch," then actually use those words when you write your notes. AI cannot find something you never named.

Let the system do the talking. Do not rewrite the AI summary from scratch unless it missed something that is factually wrong.

The entire point of this is to cut down on the time and effort it takes, not to rephrase everything by hand all over again.

Treating Meetings as Inputs Instead of Obligations

Think about how many meetings you sit through every week just to find out what happened. Not to contribute anything. Not to make a decision. Just to stay in the loop. It is one of the biggest drains on productivity in most workplaces, and it is also one of the easiest things to fix.

How to Set It Up

Start by responding to those meetings as "tentative" instead of declining them. This matters because if you decline a meeting outright, Copilot loses access to the content entirely. Marking yourself as tentative keeps you inside the permission boundary so the AI can still pull from what happened, without the meeting blocking time on your calendar.

Next, make sure transcription is turned on for meetings across your team. If your organization does not auto-transcribe meetings yet, that is the first thing to change. Whether your team runs on Teams, Zoom, or Google Meet, enable recording and transcription as the default so there is always something for the AI to work with.

Once that is in place, tell the assistant exactly which meetings to look at and which ones to skip.

Prompt: "Use only data I already have access to. Look at meetings on my calendar from the past five business days where my response status is tentative. Only include meetings where a transcript, recording, or recap is available. Do not include meetings I attended."

Then narrow the output down to only the things that actually matter to you and your work.

Prompt: "From the meetings identified above, extract only decisions, commitments, and action items that involve me directly. Do not summarize discussion. Do not include speculative or informational content."

Finally, add guardrails so the AI stays honest and does not try to fill in blanks on its own.

Prompt: "Do not infer intent, urgency, or priority. Do not assign ownership unless it is explicitly stated. If an action item or decision is unclear or incomplete, state that directly instead of filling in gaps."

To keep this system working well over time, a few small changes in how your team operates make all the difference.

Mark yourself as tentative on any meeting you are not planning to attend but still want access to. That keeps you in the loop without filling your calendar with blocks that eat into your actual work time.

Push for your organization to auto-transcribe meetings by default so there is always a record for the AI to pull from. If there is no transcript and no recap, the AI has nothing to work with and the whole system breaks down.

Make it normal for decisions and action items to be stated clearly during meetings instead of buried in side conversations or left implied. Ask teammates to say commitments out loud or drop them into the chat so that outcomes are easy to find later when the AI goes looking for them.

First Drafts Without Starting From Scratch

One of the most common places where time quietly disappears at work is the ideation phase of writing. Writing itself is not hard, but getting started always takes longer than it should. Most writing that happens at work is not creative writing; it is operational writing, the kind that follows a pattern and exists to move something forward. Proposals, statements of work, policies, project briefs, and reports all fall into this category, and every single one of them has a structure that can be built faster with the right starting point.

The good news is that you almost never have to start from nothing, even when it feels like you do.

How to Set It Up

Begin by choosing your starting material. You do not need a polished document to get going. Any of the following will work as a foundation for the AI to build from: meeting notes, a bullet point brief, past versions of similar documents, or even an email thread that contains the core details of what needs to happen. Giving the AI something real to work from helps it stay grounded in your actual situation instead of falling back on generic templates that do not match your work.

Once you have your starting material ready, use a drafting prompt that sets clear boundaries on what the AI should and should not do.

Prompt: "Use only data I already have access to. Create a first draft of a proposal or statement of work based on the attached files or the details I provide. Include standard sections such as scope, assumptions, deliverables, timeline, risks, and responsibilities. Do not invent pricing, legal terms, dates, or commitments."

After the first draft comes back, use a rewriting prompt to adjust the style and clarity until it sounds like the way you need it to.

Prompt: "Rewrite this section to be more concise while preserving meaning. Then rewrite it again in a more direct tone with fewer qualifiers. Do not change the facts, only phrasing."

Then add guardrails to make sure the AI does not overstep and start making things up to fill in gaps.

Prompt: "Do not add facts that are not present in the source material. If a section requires information that is missing, insert a bracketed placeholder that says [information needed]. Keep the tone neutral and professional. This draft is for review, not for sending."

For this whole approach to work well, a few shifts in how you think about drafting need to happen.

Treat first drafts as scaffolding, not strategy. The AI is giving you a starting structure, not a finished product. You will still need to add context, challenge what it assumed, and customize everything for your specific audience and situation.

Capture your work in formats that are easy for AI to use later. Meeting notes with clear bullet points, summaries saved in shared documents, and folders with labels that make sense all help the AI produce better drafts since it has better material to pull from.

Focus on auditing the draft instead of rewriting the whole thing from scratch. Look for gaps in the information, check the tone, and make sure it lines up with what you actually need. Do not waste time reformatting what is already close enough.

Get comfortable with bracketed placeholders showing up in your drafts. A document that says "[information needed]" in a few spots is not broken or incomplete. It is doing exactly what it should by telling you where the gaps are instead of quietly making something up to fill them.

Turning Existing Work Into Decks You Can Refine

Think about how often you end up building a slide deck for work you have already done, just to make it look "presentable" for someone else. The doc has been written. The meetings have happened. The decisions have been made. Yet when it is time to brief a stakeholder, the evening disappears into PowerPoint at 9 p.m. trying to figure out where to even start on something that should not take more than 20 minutes.

Tools like Copilot in PowerPoint, Gamma, Beautiful.ai, Tome, or even a general-purpose AI assistant with file access can handle most of this for you.

How to Set It Up

Start by choosing the source file where the real thinking already happened. This could be a Word doc or a Google Doc, a project proposal or memo, or notes from a working session or a series of meetings. The key is picking something that already contains the substance so the AI is not guessing at what you meant.

Then give the assistant clear framing so it knows exactly what to do with that material.

Prompt: "Use this document to create a presentation outline with 6 to 8 slides. Extract the key themes, decisions, and recommendations. Do not invent content. Use the language in the document as much as possible. Assume the audience is an internal stakeholder familiar with the topic but short on time."

You can also layer on additional instructions like asking it to include speaker notes or talking points, format everything in a way that is easy to copy into PowerPoint or Google Slides, or create a title slide and closing summary if those are missing from the original material.

Once the assistant generates the deck structure, your job is to check it for clarity and accuracy, adjust the flow or messaging where something feels off, and add any visuals or supporting data that will make the presentation land the way it needs to.

To keep this process repeatable and useful over time, a few small changes in how you work will make a big difference.

Write your source materials with slide readiness in mind from the start. Clear sections, clean bullet points, and well-defined themes in your documents will make every downstream automation faster and more accurate.

Label your documents with the end goal attached to them. Something as simple as "Draft Proposal, Needs Slide Version" signals to you and anyone else on your team that this document has reuse potential and is not just a one-time deliverable.

Stop treating slides as the place where the thinking starts. Use documents to think through the problem. Use AI to translate that thinking into a presentation format. Use the slides themselves to communicate what has already been decided.

Do not get caught up in making the slides look perfect on the first pass. The goal is to get 80 percent of the way there in 20 percent of the time. Visuals, formatting, and polish can all be layered in later once the structure and the message are solid.

All four of these quick wins share one thing in common. They target the kind of work that slows you down every single week but almost never shows up in your performance review. Every one of these is low risk, fast to test, and built entirely on the systems your company is already paying for.

Pick one quick win from this chapter. Set it up today and give it two full weeks before you decide whether it worked or not. Do not start a second automation until the first one has had time to settle into your routine. If you want the campaign brief template and prompt sequence to go along with this, you can download them at `http://myaiworkweek.com/campaignplaybook`.

Deciding What Should Be Automated First

Quick wins are about saving time, but game changers are about changing the nature of the work itself. You are not just speeding up a process that already exists—you are eliminating entire categories of friction that should never have been part of the workflow in the first place.

These automations take longer to build than the quick wins, but the return is exponential because they create real leverage, reduce the strain on your team without adding headcount, and make the way your organization operates permanently simpler instead of just temporarily faster.

To figure out which automations are worth the real investment of time, effort, and visibility, every idea needs to pass through a clear set of filters before anyone starts building.

The first filter is asking *whether the work is necessary or just familiar*. Strategic debt has a way of hiding in plain sight, usually buried inside the rituals and workflows that nobody ever questions simply because they have always been done that way. Here are two painful examples that show up in nearly every organization. The first is leadership manually reviewing every single sales proposal even when 90 percent of the content is identical from deal to deal, which slows down revenue and frustrates the teams who are stuck waiting for approval to move forward. The second is weekly cross-functional meetings that exist solely to align on work that already lives in tools like Asana, Notion, or Slack, meetings that only happen because teams do not trust the system of record enough to rely on it without a live conversation to confirm what they could have read for themselves.

The second filter is asking *what it costs the organization to leave the problem alone*. Sometimes the best automation opportunities are not really about saving time at all but about what is quietly being lost by doing nothing and letting the problem continue to run unchecked. Sales teams end up waiting days for custom pricing approval because the entire process lives inside someone's inbox instead of an actual system that can move without a human pushing it forward. Support teams lose momentum trying to track follow-ups across chat, email, and ticketing tools with no shared view of what has been handled and what is still sitting there waiting. Marketing handoffs stall out because getting a single brief approved takes three separate meetings just to get everyone aligned on context and goals before any real work can even begin.

The third filter is asking *whether the automation will compound over time*, meaning whether fixing this one thing will make the next improvement easier and remove complexity from the system as a whole. A good automation saves time once, but a strategic automation makes every future automation easier to build and removes layers of complexity that were slowing everything else down too. Think about what happens when every new client means re-creating onboarding workflows completely from scratch instead of triggering a reusable system that already knows the steps and the order they need to happen in. Or when each sales region develops its own version of reporting templates and training content over time, leading to drift, duplication, and inconsistent execution across the organization that only gets worse and harder to untangle as the company grows.

These are the slow bleeds that do not block anything from happening today, but they are the things that will absolutely break your ability to scale when tomorrow arrives and the volume doubles.

Now let me show you what a real game-changing automation looks like when all of these filters come together in practice. This was not a small tweak or a single workflow improvement that saved someone an hour a week. This was a system-level reset that erased entire weeks of manual effort and eliminated the chaos that had been making campaign planning reactive, scattered, and consistently late for as long as anyone on the team could remember.

It started in marketing, but not the kind of marketing you see in a brand video or a polished pitch deck at a conference. This was the messy, last minute, thrown together kind of marketing that most teams deal with constantly but never talk about publicly because it does not fit the image anyone wants to project.

Most marketing campaigns do not begin with a bold vision or a carefully crafted strategy that everyone rallied around. They start with a dry sales pipeline and a team under pressure to fix it fast. Someone checks the numbers, realizes leads are trending down, and suddenly it is all hands on deck to "get something out the door" as quickly as possible. An event gets thrown together. A webinar gets scheduled. A batch of emails gets blasted out. The team scrambles to pull it all together at the same time, writing copy, building slides, designing graphics, setting up registration forms, managing invites and follow-ups, and by the time the campaign launches, everyone involved is already burned out before they can even measure whether it worked.

Here is what a typical "simple" campaign takes inside most companies when you lay it all out. Someone has to draft the messaging from scratch. Someone else has to design the emails and landing pages to go with it. A third person has to set up the registration flow and all the reminder sequences that go along with it. Sales needs to be looped in so they know how to handle follow-up after the event happens. Data has to be tracked manually to figure out who registered, who showed up, and who disappeared without ever engaging. Every single update along the way requires a Slack message, a spreadsheet entry, or yet another meeting just to keep everyone on the same page about where things stand.

This exact work happens every single time a campaign launches, and it is almost identical from one campaign to the next with only the goals, the dates, and the specific content changing between them. People end up wasting enormous amounts of time and energy rebuilding the same house from scratch over and over again instead of focusing on the things that determine whether the campaign succeeds, which are the message, the offer, and the result it was designed to deliver. This project checked every single one of the three filters laid out earlier.

The first filter asked *whether the work was necessary or just familiar*, and the answer was painfully clear. Marketing teams everywhere run campaigns manually, not because it is the best way to do it, but because nobody has ever stopped long enough to ask whether there is a different way. It had become a habit that everyone followed without thinking, not a strategy that anyone had deliberately chosen.

The second filter asked *what it would cost to leave things the way they were*, and that cost turned out to be significant. Every campaign that got rushed out the door led to weaker leads, missed follow-ups, slower sales cycles, and constant friction between teams who were all frustrated but pointing fingers in different directions about why things kept falling apart.

The third filter asked *whether fixing this once would compound over time*, and the answer was the reason this project was worth the investment. If the architecture got built the right way one time, it could be reused for every single campaign going forward. Instead of starting over from scratch every few weeks, the team would be refining what already worked, reusing the pieces that did not need to change, and scaling the whole system without scaling the effort that went into it.

The foundation of any strong campaign is not the creative assets or the tech stack powering it. It is knowing exactly who you are talking to and what they actually care about. I do not mean in vague demographic terms like "mid-level managers in healthcare" that look good on a strategy slide but do not tell you anything useful. In real, behavioral terms that get to the heart of what drives their decisions. What do they worry about when nobody is watching? What language do they use when they describe their own problems out loud? What outcomes are they under pressure to deliver, and what happens to them personally if they fall short?

Most teams guess the answers to those questions. They sit in a conference room and brainstorm what they think the customer wants based on assumptions and past experience, then write messaging based on those assumptions and hope it lands well enough to hit the numbers. That guessing game is exactly why so many campaigns underperform despite everyone on the team working incredibly hard to make them succeed.

Instead of guessing, I let AI listen to the voice of the customer directly by going to the places where customers had already told us what they wanted in their own words. Every company is sitting on a goldmine of this kind of data without realizing it. Sales call transcripts, support tickets, survey responses, social media comments, customer reviews, and internal feedback loops all contain exactly the kind of insight that most teams spend hours in a room trying to guess at. Anywhere a customer has spoken openly about what they want, what is not working, or what matters most to them, that is raw material waiting to be used.

I feed all of that aggregated information into AI and ask for something simple.

Prompt: "What pain points show up the most across this data? What objections come up again and again? What outcomes do people celebrate when things go right?"

In just a few minutes, what comes back is a ranked list of what matters most, not to me and not to the marketing team, but to the audience the campaign is trying to reach. Their language is right there on the screen. Their priorities are laid out clearly. The disconnect between what I thought was important and what they are struggling with becomes impossible to ignore. That is the real beginning of the campaign, and everything else that gets built from that point forward is grounded in something real instead of something assumed.

Once the customer is understood at that level, the next step is defining exactly what the campaign needs them to do in specific, measurable terms that leave no room for vague interpretations of success. Get 100 qualified leads to register for a webinar. Drive 50 demo requests from target accounts within 30 days. Convert 20 percent of attendees into sales conversations within one week of the event. When the goal is that specific and that measurable, everything else clicks into place naturally because every decision from that point forward can be tested against whether it moves that number or does not. You are not just "running a campaign" anymore. You are building a system that is deliberately designed to produce a specific result.

Most campaigns fall apart in the execution phase, which is where creative thinking gives way to pure grunt work that nobody enjoys but everybody accepts as unavoidable. Someone has to write five emails. Someone has to build a landing page. Someone has to draft LinkedIn posts and script follow-up messages for the people who registered but did not show up. Someone has to set up reminder workflows inside the email platform and coordinate with sales on exactly who is responsible for what once the leads start coming in. Every single one of those tasks gets done from scratch every single time a new campaign launches, even though the structure is nearly identical to the last one. That is not creative work by any definition. It is patterned work that follows the same sequence every time, which makes it a perfect candidate for the kind of automation that can change how an entire team operates.

Here is the exact workflow I used to rebuild the campaign system from the ground up. The first step is creating the campaign brief, which is a single document that contains five things: the goal, the target audience, the core message, the offer which is whatever you are giving people in exchange for taking action, and the timeline for the whole campaign. This takes about 20 minutes of focused thinking to put together, but those 20 minutes replace hours of wandering conversations later where everyone is trying to figure out what the campaign is actually supposed to accomplish.

The second step is handing that brief to AI with a structured prompt that tells it exactly what to build.

Prompt: "Create a full campaign plan for this brief. Include a five-part email sequence, a landing page outline, three LinkedIn posts, and follow-up messaging for people who register and people who do not. Use the audience language and pain points from our earlier analysis. Keep the tone consistent with our brand. Make sure every message ties back to the core goal."

Twenty minutes later, what comes back is not a rough draft or a loose outline that needs hours of reworking. It is a polished, structured plan that is ready to execute with only minor adjustments needed to make it feel exactly right.

The third step is validating those AI-generated insights against real-world data before jumping into content creation. I wanted to make sure that what the AI surfaced was not just accurate but also current and reflective of what was happening in the market right now. So I ran everything through a data enrichment layer using a tool like Clay, which connects directly to public sources like LinkedIn, company websites, job boards, and other places where real buyer behavior is visible.

Here is what that looked like in practice. I used it to confirm that the job titles and industries the AI identified actually matched our target profile. I pulled recent LinkedIn activity from people in our target audience to see what topics were trending in their space and what conversations they were already having. I checked whether the common objections that kept showing up in past sales calls also appeared in buyer-facing content and discussions happening online. I also verified contact-level data that would matter for lead routing and scoring later on, things like company size, tech stack, and hiring trends that signal whether a company is likely to be in buying mode.

This step gave me a way to pressure-test everything the AI had surfaced in the earlier steps. If the AI told me that "integration complexity" was a top objection but the real customer profiles showed that most of them were using simple plug-and-play tools, I knew there was a mismatch that needed to be corrected before any messaging went out. If LinkedIn posts from people in my target audience were echoing the exact same pain points the AI had flagged, I knew we were on the right track and could move forward with confidence.

The fourth step is generating all of the campaign assets in one workspace instead of bouncing between a dozen different tabs and tools. With the messaging locked in and the insights validated, it was time to build the actual materials, and I did it all using the Canva integration inside ChatGPT so that the move from strategy to visuals happened in one seamless flow.

I used it to generate polished email layouts that matched our brand guidelines and highlighted a single clear call to action in each one. I created social media posts and graphics specifically designed for LinkedIn, complete with copy, hashtags, and visuals tailored to the target persona we had built earlier. I built landing page mockups that were structured around the customer's pain points, the specific offer, and the campaign timeline so that every element on the page had a reason for being there.

The best part of working this way is that I never had to explain the campaign from scratch to a new tool or start over in a different window. I simply referenced the brief that had already been created earlier in the conversation, and ChatGPT carried all of that context forward into every new asset it generated. I would say things like "Create a LinkedIn post that summarizes the campaign in plain language and uses a customer quote to drive urgency" and within minutes there was usable content on the screen ready to go. From there, I made small adjustments to polish the language or swap out a visual, but at no point was anything being created from a blank page.

The fifth step is automating the actual campaign execution directly from inside ChatGPT. Once the campaign assets were ready, including all of the emails, social posts, and landing pages, it was time to connect everything to our marketing platform and make it run intelligently based on how people were engaging, not just on a fixed schedule that treated everyone the same way regardless of their behavior. I used integrations directly inside the workspace to connect the campaign to platforms like HubSpot and asked ChatGPT to define the lead scoring criteria based on real intent signals.

Prompt: "Create a scoring model for this webinar campaign. Assign points based on opens, clicks, attendance, and form responses. Cap at 100."

The sixth and final step is analyzing what happened, learning from it, and improving while the campaign is still running instead of waiting until it is over. Once the campaign launched, there was no shift into "wait and see" mode where everyone crosses their fingers and checks back in a week later. Instead, the shift was into optimize-and-adapt mode, and all of it happened inside ChatGPT by using the Google Analytics plug-in to ask plain-language questions and get real insights without having to log in to a separate dashboard or manually build reports in a spreadsheet.

Here are the kinds of questions that got asked along the way: "Which landing page section had the highest drop-off this week?" and "What traffic source converted best over the last three days?" and "Which emails had the lowest click-through rate, and what might improve them?" ChatGPT gave back answers that could be acted on immediately without waiting for a weekly report to land or spending an afternoon wrangling data into a format that made sense.

The campaign launched on a Monday morning. By Friday of that first week, there were 50 registrations. By the end of the second week, that number had climbed to 80. By the end of the month, the campaign had produced 92 qualified leads and 14 booked demos. The follow-up was entirely automated from start to finish. Attendees received one sequence designed for people who showed up and engaged. No shows received a completely different sequence designed to reengage them and bring them back. High engagement prospects were automatically flagged for immediate sales outreach so that no warm lead sat untouched while someone manually sorted through a spreadsheet trying to figure out who to call first. The entire system ran without a single manual email being sent.

If you want to see exactly how I structured my time audit along with the campaign brief template and the prompt sequence I used to build this entire system, I have published anonymized versions of both that you can download at `http://myaiworkweek.com/campaignplaybook`.

The entire campaign was designed and built in under 5 hours from start to finish. All of the emails, landing pages, and social media posts were generated inside ChatGPT using the Canva integration without ever leaving the workspace. Smart lead scoring, personalized sequences, and automated reminders were all set up and launched directly from inside ChatGPT connected to the marketing platform. Performance summaries came back in plain language through ChatGPT paired with the Google Analytics plug-in, which meant no logging in to dashboards and no building reports from scratch. There were no spreadsheets to maintain, no handoffs to coordinate between teams, and no time wasted chasing people down to find out where things stood.

AI Automation for Knowledge Workers

Across every team, knowledge workers are already automating the parts of their jobs that used to eat up their time, slow down their decisions, or pull them away from work that actually matters. These are not ideas for someday. They are real things happening right now inside tools that most teams already use.

Think about how often your day gets interrupted by looking for something you know exists. The document is out there somewhere. You remember the decision being made. You can picture the slide in your head. You just cannot for the life of you remember where it ended up. So you check email first, then try chat, then dig through a shared drive, and then maybe open up the CRM hoping someone saved it there. What should take a few seconds turns into minutes, and those minutes add up to hours every single week that nobody ever gets back. Most teams just accept this as normal because it has always been this way and nobody has ever stopped to ask if there is a better option.

When AI is connected across your systems, the whole experience feels different. Instead of opening five different tools and clicking through folders trying to hunt something down, you just ask a question in plain language like "Where is the onboarding guide for customer success managers?" The system does not just hand you 10 links and leave you to figure out which one is right. It pulls up the correct document, gives you a short summary of what is in it, and drops a direct link to the source so you can check it yourself. The whole thing stops feeling like a treasure hunt and starts feeling more like asking a coworker who happens to remember where everything is.

The way this works behind the scenes is that a search layer connects all of your main systems together, including email, calendar, chat, shared drives, knowledge bases, ticketing tools, and your CRM. Tools like Glean, Read AI, Guru, Google Cloud Search, or Vertex AI Search can scan content across all of those systems while making sure that every person only sees what they already have permission to see. Nothing leaks where it should not.

Getting this set up starts with being clear about what problems you are trying to solve. Pick three to five questions that your team struggles to answer quickly on a regular basis and focus on the ones tied to money, risk, or decisions that cannot sit around waiting. Choose a search tool that connects easily with what your company already uses, hook up your systems, let the tool scan and organize your content in the background, and then show your team how to ask questions in plain language instead of digging through folders and threads on their own.

What you get out of this is not just faster searching, even though that alone makes a huge difference. You get faster decisions across the board, and when decisions happen faster, everything else starts moving faster too.

Here is how to set it up step by step, assuming your team works in something like product, consulting, or operations and you are rolling out a search tool like Glean or Read AI alongside Copilot and Gemini.

Start by figuring out your core use cases. Write down three to five questions that people on your team cannot get quick answers to right now, things like "Show me the onboarding docs for new customer success managers" or "What was the final pricing decision from last quarter?" Put the questions that waste the most time and have the biggest impact on the business at the top of the list, especially the ones where delayed answers lead to stalled decisions, overlooked risks, or revenue that sits on hold while someone hunts for information.

Then choose your AI search tool based on what your company already runs on. If your team uses Google Workspace and a handful of other software tools, Google Cloud Search or Vertex AI Search are solid choices, or you could go with something like Glean that already has built in connections to most of the tools you are using every day. Make sure Copilot and Gemini are part of the setup too so that your team has more than one way to tap into the same information. If your team relies heavily on what gets said in meetings, which is common in sales and consulting, take a look at Read AI for deep recall across meetings, emails, and documents and pair it with Copilot and Gemini for even more context.

Next, connect your main systems by turning on the connectors for email whether that is Gmail or Outlook; your calendar; chat tools like Slack or Teams; shared drives like Google Drive, OneDrive, or SharePoint; and whatever knowledge bases your team depends on like Confluence, Notion, internal wikis, or your CRM. Make sure the tool you pick respects the permissions that are already in place so that people only ever see what they are supposed to see and nothing crosses a boundary it should not.

After that, let the tool start scanning and organizing your content, which usually happens quietly in the background without disrupting anyone's day. Once the scanning is underway, test it by having people from different teams run the same search and comparing what comes back. Someone from HR should see different results than someone from Sales for the same question, and if that is not happening, the permissions need to be adjusted before you go any further.

Set up the system so that when someone searches for something, they get an answer with a link to the source instead of just a pile of documents to sort through on their own. Turn on conversational search so people can type questions the way they would ask a coworker and get a clear response with the most important details pulled out and a direct link to where the information originally came from. Add Copilot and Gemini summaries on top of that so users get even more context without needing to open every single document themselves.

Build the search experience into the tools your team already lives in so it becomes a natural part of how they work instead of one more thing to remember. Add a shortcut or slash command in Slack or Teams, something like `/search-pricing-decision`, so people can look something up without leaving the conversation they are already in. Put a search bar or AI assistant on your company's internal homepage so people can start their day by getting answers to whatever is on their mind right away.

Help your team get started by sharing example questions directly in Slack or Teams that people can copy, paste, and use immediately without having to figure out the right way to phrase things on their own. Include ready-made prompts for Copilot and Gemini so there is zero guesswork involved and everyone can see value from day one.

Once the system is running, keep track of how it is performing and make it better over time. Look at things like how often searches return a useful answer, how long it takes people to find what they need, and which teams are using it the most versus which ones might need a little more encouragement. Talk to the people on your team who are getting the most out of it and use what they tell you to fine-tune which content gets prioritized, whether certain areas like product specs or project playbooks need to show up higher in results, and where the experience still has room to improve. Set up feedback loops for Copilot and Gemini so the whole system keeps getting better based on how your team uses it day to day.

Every team has lived through the moment where a meeting starts and someone asks, "What did we decide last time?" and the next 15 minutes disappear while people scroll through old messages or argue about what they think they remember. All the context from the last conversation has to be rebuilt from scratch before anyone can talk about what comes next, and by the time everyone is finally caught up, half the meeting is already gone.

The real cost of that moment goes beyond the time that gets wasted looking for information that should be easy to find. It is the way confidence slowly falls apart when nobody on the team feels sure about what was already agreed on, which makes every conversation after that slower and more cautious than it needs to be.

AI fixes this by pulling together information that used to be scattered across a dozen different places. Meeting notes, emails, support tickets, and documents all get organized into one timeline where decisions have dates next to them, open questions are clearly marked, and links to the original sources are right there so anyone who wants to double-check something can do it in seconds.

Picture opening your next meeting with a summary already on the screen showing the last three decisions that were made, the thinking behind each one, and the items that are still open and waiting for someone to act on them. The conversation jumps straight into what matters instead of spending the first 20 minutes trying to reconstruct what happened last time, and the team gets to spend their energy debating what to do next instead of arguing about what already happened.

To make this work, connect your calendar, meeting transcripts, email, ticketing tools, and document storage to a work AI platform that can bring all of that information together in one place. Set up consistent naming and tagging for your projects so the system can automatically group related content and pull it up when someone asks about a specific initiative. Create simple prompts like "Summarize the latest decisions and open questions for Project Apollo with dates and links" and save those prompts somewhere the whole team can get to them easily, especially right before recurring meetings where rebuilding context has always been the biggest waste of time.

Instant Project and Decision History

Every team has lived through the moment where a meeting starts and someone asks, "What did we decide last time?" and the next 15 minutes vanish while people scroll through old messages or argue about what they think they remember. All the context from the last conversation has to be rebuilt from scratch before anyone can move forward, and by the time everyone is finally caught up, half the meeting is already gone.

The real cost is the way confidence slowly falls apart when nobody feels sure about what was already agreed on, which makes every conversation after that slower and more careful than it needs to be.

AI can fix this by pulling together information that used to live in a dozen different places and organizing it into one clear picture. Meeting notes, emails, support tickets, and documents all get stitched into a single timeline where decisions have dates next to them, open questions are clearly called out, and links to the original sources are right there for anyone who wants to double-check.

Imagine opening your next meeting with a summary already on the screen showing what was decided, why it was decided, and what still needs attention. Instead of spending the first 20 minutes looking backward, the team jumps straight into what matters and spends their energy on what to do next rather than rehashing what already happened.

How to Set It Up

Hook up your core sources first by linking your calendar, meeting tools like Zoom or Teams, email, ticketing platforms, and shared drive documents to your AI platform so it can see the full picture of everything that has been happening around a given project.

Next, set up tagging rules so the system can group related content on its own. Use project-level tags like "Project-Apollo" or "Q2-Launch" the same way across every tool so that when someone asks about a specific initiative, the AI pulls in the right meetings, emails, documents, and tickets without mixing in things that do not belong.

Then create go to prompts that your team can use at the top of any meeting without having to figure out how to ask the question each time.

Prompt: "Summarize the latest decisions and open questions for [project name], with dates and links to the original sources."

Put those prompts somewhere everyone can grab them quickly, whether that is pinned in your AI assistant, bookmarked in Slack or

Teams, or dropped right into the recurring meeting agenda so they are always waiting when the conversation begins.

Faster Onboarding for New Hires

The first few weeks in a new role almost always feel like drinking from a firehose. New hires end up relying on whatever bits of knowledge they can pick up from the people around them, interrupting coworkers with questions that nobody has time to answer properly, and trying to piece together how things work from scattered documents that may or may not still be accurate. How fast someone gets up to speed usually depends on who happens to be free to help them that day, which is not a real system. It is luck.

Most companies do not think of slow onboarding as a serious business problem, but it hits revenue, execution speed, and team morale in ways that pile up quickly. Every week a new hire spends confused and trying to figure things out is a week of full salary going toward someone who is not yet able to do the job they were brought in to do. Every question that pulls a senior team member away from their own priorities has a hidden cost too, even if nobody is keeping track.

When AI is connected to your knowledge systems, onboarding becomes something structured and repeatable instead of something that gets made up on the fly every time a new person joins. Instead of handing someone a giant list of links and hoping for the best, you define the topics that matter most for their specific role ahead of time and point the AI at the documents that hold the real answers. From there, the system can walk new hires through what they need to know in a logical order, answer their questions with direct links to approved sources, and surface the same questions that previous new hires asked so the same ground does not have to be covered from scratch every single time.

How to Set It Up

Start by identifying the must know topics for each role, usually somewhere between 5 and 10 core areas that every new hire in that position needs to understand, things like key metrics, daily processes, team playbooks, and decision frameworks that guide how the work gets done.

Then pin the authoritative documents for each of those topics so the AI knows which sources to treat as the definitive answers. This is what keeps the system from pulling in outdated drafts or random notes that someone forgot to delete and pointing new hires in the wrong direction.

Build a centralized onboarding space inside whatever knowledge platform your team already uses and let the AI generate a learning path for each role that includes links to the right documents, quick knowledge checks, and a clear sequence so that new hires know exactly what to read first and what can wait until later.

Encourage every new hire to ask their questions through the system instead of only reaching out to teammates through direct messages. Every question that gets asked and answered through the platform makes the knowledge base stronger and better prepared for the next person who starts, which means onboarding gets a little smoother every single time without anyone having to do extra work to make that happen.

Client Account Briefing in One Question

Now think about a different kind of pressure that shows up almost every week for anyone in a client-facing role. That moment an hour before a big call when you are scrambling to pull together everything you need to walk in prepared. You open the CRM to check the latest notes. You scan through recent emails looking for anything important. You dig through support tickets to make sure nothing is on fire. You search the shared drive hoping the most recent version of the proposal deck is somewhere you can actually find it. Preparation turns into a race against the clock, and even when you do everything right, there is always a chance you missed something critical that was hiding in a system you forgot to check.

When AI connects your CRM data, communication history, ticketing systems, and shared drives together, preparation goes from being a frantic scavenger hunt to something that takes seconds. Instead of gathering pieces from five different places and trying to assemble the picture yourself, you simply ask for a briefing. Within moments you get a clear summary of the last several interactions with that client, any open issues or support tickets, the financial value of the relationship, potential risks on the horizon, and direct links to every supporting document you might need during the conversation. You walk into the meeting informed and ready instead of rushed and hoping you did not miss anything.

How to Set It Up

Connect your CRM platform, whether that is Salesforce or HubSpot or something else, alongside email, calendar, support tools, and document drives to your AI layer so that it has visibility into everything related to a given client or account. Set up account-level groupings so that all of the emails, tickets, documents, and meeting notes associated with a specific client or opportunity get tied together automatically instead of floating around in separate systems with no connection between them. Create a standard briefing prompt that anyone on the team can use before a client meeting.

Prompt: "Generate a one-page briefing for this account, including the last five interactions, any open tickets, financial value, current risks, and links to supporting documents."

Put access to this briefing directly inside the CRM interface or in the calendar sidebar so it becomes a natural part of how people prepare instead of an extra step they have to remember. When preparation is this easy and this consistent, risk goes down, nothing important gets missed, and every client conversation becomes more strategic because the person walking in knows the full picture before they say a word.

Think about how much of your day goes toward finding information instead of using it. You know the document exists but cannot remember where it lives. You sat through the meeting where the decision was made but now nobody can agree on what was decided. You spend 20 minutes before every client call pulling together context from five different tools just to feel prepared. None of that creates value. It just prevents things from falling apart.

That friction has been part of work for so long that it feels normal now. Everyone deals with it. Nobody questions it. When AI removes it, something shifts that is hard to put back. Your day feels lighter without the workload actually shrinking. Meetings start with clarity instead of a 15-minute scramble to get everyone caught up. Decisions happen faster because the context behind them shows up the moment someone needs it. For the first time in a long time, there is room in the day to stop and think.

That room matters more than the speed. Most people think AI is valuable because it makes work faster. It does, but that is only the beginning. The real question is what you do with the mental space that opens up once the busywork stops swallowing every hour. Some people will use it to check more boxes before lunch and call it a win. Others will step back far enough to see patterns they have been missing, connect work happening across teams that nobody else is linking together, and start walking into rooms with perspective instead of just information.

There is a risk hiding in here, too. If everyone eventually gets the same tools and the same time savings, productivity becomes the baseline. It stops being the thing that makes anyone stand out. Efficiency alone will not be enough when AI is built into the systems that every person in your company uses every day.

What separates you from everyone else is what you do with the time and clarity those tools give back. Do you fill the space with more tasks, or do you use it to get strategic about where your energy goes? Do you let AI make your execution smoother and stop there, or do you use it to change how the people making decisions about your career see your work?

That question is the bridge into what comes next. Everything up to this point has been about taking friction out of the systems around you, and you now have a foundation underneath you that most professionals are still trying to figure out.

The next chapter goes somewhere different. It is about what happens when you stop using that foundation just to work faster and start using it to grow your visibility, strengthen your influence, and build the kind of career that does not collapse the moment one tool or one trend moves on without you. The focus shifts from systems to positioning, from getting things done to making sure the right people know what you have done and why it mattered.

Chapter 4

Multiplication Effect

You know the feeling that creeps in when headlines start shouting about AI taking jobs: Every week there is another article warning that automation is cutting roles, that tools are outperforming people, or that companies are saving money by letting machines do what humans used to do.

For anyone who has spent years building a career, it is completely natural to wonder whether the ground is shifting underneath them. That fear makes sense. It is also missing a big piece of the picture.

AI is getting rid of manual work. It is shrinking the time spent on repetitive tasks, searching for information, drafting documents, summarizing meetings, and building things that follow a predictable pattern.

What it is not getting rid of is the need for someone to make the hard calls, set the direction, interpret what the data actually means, and make sure the whole system is working the way it should.

In a lot of organizations, the opposite of job loss is happening right now. As the routine tasks shrink, entirely new roles are showing up that did not exist a few years ago, roles built around managing, guiding, and scaling these systems responsibly.

Look at the job market over the past 2 years and you will see titles that most people had never heard of before:

- AI Product Manager
- Prompt Engineer
- AI Workflow Architect
- Automation Strategist
- AI Operations Lead
- Human in the Loop Reviewer
- AI Trainer
- Knowledge Orchestration Manager
- Model Risk Analyst
- AI Governance Lead
- Digital Workforce Manager

Not a single one of those roles replaces a human. Every one of them exists because humans are needed to shape how AI gets used, watched, improved, and connected to real business outcomes.

When spreadsheets showed up, bookkeepers did not disappear. Financial analysts emerged instead. When the Internet changed how people bought things, it did not erase marketers. It created entirely new fields like digital marketing, growth strategy, search engine optimization (SEO), and analytics. Technology does not just subtract jobs from the world—it reorganizes how work gets done and creates new kinds of work in the process.

Right now, as this book is being written, there is a live example running in the background that proves this point perfectly. A tool called Clawdbot is connected to my website and takes instructions through text messages. It fixes broken components, adjusts layouts, cleans up small inconsistencies, and asks clarifying questions when something is unclear. Work that used to require hours of back and forth with a developer now gets compressed into a few minutes of guided conversation.

Has it eliminated work? Without question. Manual editing, repetitive debugging, and routine front-end fixes take a fraction of the time they used to. Has it eliminated the need for someone to oversee what it does? Not even close.

Someone still has to define what the end result should look like. Someone still has to review every change before it goes live. Someone still has to decide whether what the tool produced actually fits the brand, the user experience, and the broader strategy. On top of all that, there is now an entirely new layer of work that did not exist before this tool showed up. Training it. Refining the prompts that guide it. Setting boundaries around what it should and should not touch. Watching the outputs for mistakes. Knowing when to trust the automation and when to step in and override it.

That is brand-new work that was created, not eliminated, by bringing AI into the process. Getting rid of the manual effort opened up space, and the real question is what organizations choose to do with that space once they have it.

The companies thinking ahead are not just pocketing the savings and doing less. They are putting that recovered time back into things that grow the business, like designing better customer experiences, going deeper on analytics and insight, running experiments faster, communicating with clients before problems show up instead of after, and getting teams across departments to work together in ways that were never possible when everyone was buried in busywork.

At the individual level, the same shift matters just as much. When AI saves you 5 hours a week, the question that determines everything is what happens to those 5 hours. If they get swallowed up by more low-value tasks and more reactive busywork, nothing about your situation changes. If they get redirected into work that requires your judgment, your creativity, and your ability to see the bigger picture, everything changes.

This is where training and time management become critical parts of the conversation. The organizations getting the most out of AI are not just installing tools and hoping for the best. They are teaching their people how to manage the time those tools free up. They are helping teams figure out which parts of their work genuinely require a human brain and which parts do not. They are redesigning how work flows through the organization based on what people are capable of instead of what they have always done out of habit.

The smartest companies are already asking a new set of questions that most organizations have not gotten to yet. What should our people stop doing entirely because a machine can handle it? What should they supervise instead of doing themselves? Where should the saved time be reinvested to create the most value? How do we train our teams to think in terms of systems and outcomes instead of individual tasks and checklists?

The work that requires hands-on execution is becoming assisted by machines. The work that requires direction, judgment, and the ability to connect the dots across an organization is becoming more critical than it has ever been.

The real risk here is not that AI will wipe out all jobs. The risk is that people hold on tightly to the parts of their role that are the easiest to automate because those are the parts that feel familiar and safe. When your value at work is defined purely by how well you execute tasks, automation feels like a direct threat to your livelihood. When your value is defined by how well you interpret information, set priorities, and make sure everything is aligned toward the right goals, automation stops being a threat and starts being something that makes you more powerful at the things only you can do.

This is where the multiplier mindset becomes essential. Multipliers do not try to compete with AI on speed or volume—they use it. They put it to work increasing their output, sharpening their communication, and making their thinking clearer and more visible to the people around them. They understand that as the baseline level of productivity rises across the board because everyone has access to the same tools, the thing that sets one person apart from another shifts away from how much they produce and toward how clearly they can connect what they produce to outcomes that matter.

In nearly every company, what gets rewarded is not just work that gets completed but work that gets connected to something bigger. Leaders are not sitting around wishing they had more activity updates from their teams. What they lack is someone who can take all of that activity and turn it into a clear story about what is working, what is not, and what should happen next. As AI strips away more and more of the manual layers that used to fill everyone's day, the professionals who come out ahead will be the ones who can translate raw execution into real insight that other people can act on.

The future of work is not getting smaller. It is getting reorganized from the ground up. The question is no longer whether tasks are going to be automated because many of them already have been. The real question is whether you are going to evolve alongside that change or dig in and resist it until the choice is no longer yours to make.

When manual work shrinks, the things that matter most are visibility, alignment, judgment, and the ability to influence the people and decisions around you. That is exactly where this conversation is headed next.

Becoming a Multiplier

If you want to understand how to do this, start by studying how your executives communicate. Watch how they present to the company, to the board, and to their peers. Pay attention to the rhythm of their updates and notice what gets the most airtime. What do they emphasize and what do they blow right past?

Some leaders zero in on revenue and margin above everything else. Others spend most of their energy talking about risk or customer retention. A few rely on storytelling to drive their points home, while others move quickly through hard numbers and expect the room to keep up.

None of that is random. The way a leader communicates reveals how they process information and how they decide what matters. When you learn to match your own communication to that style, you take the friction out of their decision making and make it dramatically easier for them to understand and act on what you are bringing to them.

AI can speed up this learning curve in a big way. Feed it a transcript from an executive presentation or an all-hands meeting and ask what themes keep showing up. Which key performance indicators (KPIs) get mentioned the most? What kinds of questions come up again and again? How does the speaker move from one topic to the next?

Those answers give you a clear map of how that person thinks, and once you have that map, framing your own updates in their language becomes almost second nature. You stop sounding like someone checking boxes and start sounding like a strategic partner who sees the business through the same lens they do.

This shift shows up even more clearly in the everyday communication that most people barely think about. Weekly updates, the kind that land in inboxes every Friday afternoon, quietly shape how leaders see the people around them over time. Those impressions get built through consistency, clarity, and how well someone connects their day-to-day work to what the company is trying to accomplish.

An update that just lists what got done blends into the background and gets skimmed or ignored. One that ties those same tasks to revenue impact, cost savings, risk reduction, or progress on a strategic priority jumps off the screen. The actual work might be identical in both versions. How it gets framed is what changes the perception, and perception is what opens doors.

AI helps here not by inflating what you did but by making the connection between your work and the outcome it supported easier to see and easier to say. It can compare your updates to the company's stated goals and flag where the link is strong versus where it is missing. It can suggest ways to reword the same information so it ties more directly to measurable results instead of just describing tasks.

Over weeks and months, those small adjustments compound into something much bigger than any single update. Leaders start connecting your name with clear thinking, sharp foresight, and the kind of alignment that makes their own decisions easier.

Multiplication does not stop at how you communicate either. It reaches into how you build and hold onto relationships across the organization. Recognition moves in every direction inside a company, and people remember who took the time to make them feel noticed.

Small moments stack up into real trust over time in ways most people drastically underestimate. A colleague mentions a milestone they care about. Someone shares a preference or a personal detail that matters to them. In a normal week, that kind of information vanishes into the noise and gets forgotten before the next meeting starts. AI can help you hang onto those details by keeping track of preferences, anniversaries, interests, and context from past conversations so that when the right moment shows up, you have something genuine to offer instead of a forgettable response.

This is not about being calculated or playing some kind of game. It is about choosing to pay attention on purpose in a world where almost everyone is too buried to do it well.

In workplaces that feel more transactional and impersonal by the day, being the person who genuinely remembers builds influence that no title or promotion can match. Trust grows quietly over months and years in ways that are hard to measure but impossible to fake. Collaboration gets smoother because people naturally want to work with someone who treats them like a real person instead of just another name on a task board. Your network across the company strengthens not because you are working the room but because you are paying real attention to the people in it.

Something important becomes very clear at this point: The real threat was never automation. The real threat has always been staying stuck in the parts of your role that a machine can do just as well or better.

When your value at work comes down to how efficiently you execute tasks, every new tool that speeds things up feels like it is quietly replacing you piece by piece. When your value comes from how well you read a situation, how tightly you connect your work to what the business needs most, and how reliable your judgment is when things get complicated, every one of those same tools turns into something that makes you stronger instead of weaker.

One caution is worth raising here, though. Multiplication without focus creates something that looks like progress from the outside but is really just noise. Becoming more visible without also pulling back from low-value work puts you at risk of being seen as someone who shows up everywhere but never actually moves the needle on anything important. Leaders do not hand out recognition for being in constant motion. What gets rewarded is leverage, the ability to create outsized results from tightly focused effort.

As routine tasks keep shrinking, the smart move is not to replace them with more activity just to stay busy. The smart move is getting ruthless about subtraction. What deserves to be fully automated so no person ever has to touch it again? What should be handed to someone else because it does not need your judgment or your experience? What should just stop happening entirely because it never delivered enough value to earn the time it took?

Knowing what to cut is just as powerful as knowing what to grow. That is where this conversation heads next, because once you know how to elevate your role, the real challenge becomes rebuilding your workload so it reflects that elevation instead of dragging you back into old patterns.

As your responsibilities expand, multiplication itself starts to look different. Managing your own work with AI makes you faster. Managing other people with AI makes you smarter about where to direct their energy. Reaching the level where you manage the people who manage others changes the question entirely. It stops being about speed or even productivity and becomes about design.

At that level, what you produce is not a report or a campaign or a feature. What you produce is the environment where other people create those things. You are setting the incentives that shape behavior, establishing the rituals that give the work its rhythm, defining the expectations that tell everyone what good looks like, and deciding how success gets measured and discussed. AI stops giving you leverage over tasks and starts giving you leverage over structure, which is where culture takes root inside an organization.

Most leaders blow right past this moment without realizing what it means. New AI tools get rolled out, efficiency numbers go up, the wins get celebrated at the next company meeting, and everyone moves on. Something far more significant is happening underneath all of that, though. As execution becomes easier for everyone with access to these tools, the ability to exercise genuinely good judgment becomes rarer and more valuable by the day. As information floods in from every direction, the ability to cut through it all and deliver clarity becomes the scarcest thing in the building.

A leader managing other managers becomes a true multiplier right at this intersection. The question stops being whether teams are busy, because busy is easy to achieve when the tools handle most of the heavy lifting. The question that actually matters is whether those teams are aimed at the right problems, because pointing productive people at the wrong target is one of the most expensive mistakes an organization can make.

Measuring activity gives way to measuring consequence, meaning what actually changed in the business as a direct result of the work that got done. Saying that out loud makes it sound like a subtle distinction, but in practice it transforms how a team operates and what it becomes capable of delivering.

Two experiments bring this to life in a way that shifts real behavior without feeling like another dreaded operational audit.

Decision Quality Review

The first is what I call the decision quality review. Instead of looking at output volume, pull your managers together and examine the last five major decisions their teams made. Product bets. Hiring calls. Budget allocations. Customer concessions. For each one, ask a straightforward set of questions. What information did we rely on? Which assumptions turned out to be wrong? Where did we move too slowly and lose an opportunity? Where did we charge ahead without enough signal to justify the risk?

Bring AI into that reflection by feeding meeting transcripts and supporting documents into the system and asking it to find patterns. Where does the team consistently hesitate? What blind spots keep reappearing? Which signals were available but got overlooked?

More often than not, what comes back is uncomfortable. Repeated optimism that blocked the team from acknowledging real risk. A habit of dismissing what customers were clearly saying. Internal preferences consistently winning out over external evidence. Surfacing those patterns is not about multiplying effort anymore. It is about multiplying the quality of every decision the organization makes going forward, which is where the real leverage sits at this level.

Capability Mapping

The second experiment replaces traditional headcount planning with capability mapping. The default approach to growing a team has always been asking whether more people are needed. A multiplier at this level asks something completely different, which is what capabilities the organization needs more of and which of those can be strengthened through AI instead of through another hire.

Map each manager's team by capability instead of job title. Strategy. Analysis. Relationship management. Creative thinking. Technical execution. Then look at where AI meaningfully amplifies each area and where human nuance still dominates. In some clusters, AI lets a small team punch well above its weight. In others, the human element is irreplaceable and no tool comes close to matching what a skilled person brings.

Hiring decisions look completely different through this lens. Instead of bringing people on to handle more execution, you start hiring for judgment, cross-functional fluency, and the kind of thinking that connects what is happening in one corner of the business to everything else.

That ripple changes how managers develop their teams, what skills get celebrated, and what earns someone a promotion. You are no longer managing tasks or even people in the traditional sense. You are deliberately shaping the mix of human and machine capabilities across the organization and making intentional choices about what combination gives your teams the best shot at winning.

That is a fundamentally different kind of leadership. The multiplication happening at this level is quieter on a daily basis but carries far more weight over time. You are shaping how your organization thinks, not just how it operates. You are tipping the balance from mindless activity toward genuine insight. You are building environments where good decisions become the natural outcome instead of the lucky exception.

This is the point where the fear of AI replacing people finally runs out of oxygen. Operating at the level of judgment, direction, and system design means automation does not chip away at your relevance. It sharpens everything you already bring to the table and makes it more valuable than it has ever been.

Routine work will keep getting smaller. Nothing is going to reverse that trend. What will keep growing is the demand for people who can design how work gets done, steer teams through uncertainty, make sense of what the numbers are really saying, and lift the performance of everyone around them.

The multiplier is not the person who squeezes the most output from AI. The multiplier is the person who ensures every team, every manager, and every initiative is aimed at something that genuinely matters and has what it needs to get there. When you reach that place, your value has nothing to do with what you personally produce anymore. It lives in what becomes possible when you are in the room, and that is the one thing no machine is built to replace.

Three-Phase Reduction

Before we get into reduction, I want you to do something that might feel uncomfortable: Write down your goals. Not the quarterly objectives sitting in your performance plan. Your real ones.

Where do you see yourself in 5 years? What kind of life are you building toward? What does a normal Tuesday look like in that life? What kind of work fills your day and what kind of work is nowhere near it? What does your relationship with your family look like when you are not constantly distracted or exhausted? How much flexibility do you have over your own schedule? How much pressure are you carrying around that you have just learned to live with?

I am not turning this into a motivational book. I am grounding you in something that matters more than any tool or tactic in these pages.

You are going to get time back. If you use AI well, the inefficient parts of your role will shrink or disappear entirely. Work that used to take hours will get compressed into minutes. Mental energy that used to get burned on repetition will open up for something better.

Here is the part most people miss, though. If you do not decide in advance what that freed up space is for, someone else will decide for you, and it will get swallowed by more meetings, more requests, and more of the same invisible work that was draining you before any of this started.

I learned this the hard way. After about 2 years of being the person pushing AI inside my role, it became clear that my capacity had grown well beyond what it used to be. The traditional schedule was still in place, but the actual execution time inside that schedule had shrunk dramatically.

Instead of letting that extra space fill up with more internal requests and other people's emergencies, a plan started to take shape. Building something independent had always been the goal, but sudden high-risk leaps have never been a good fit for how I operate. Big dramatic transitions create anxiety, not momentum. So the path forward had to be gradual and intentional.

A newsletter came first. Then a commitment to learning in public and sharing what was working. The reclaimed time got invested in small, consistent pieces instead of one big bet. Within 5 months, it had grown into something real. Monetization got tested next through lessons and courses that proved people were willing to pay for what was being taught. There was no dramatic resignation. No grand exit story. Just a steady, deliberate build toward having options that did not exist before.

A few years ago, that kind of parallel build alongside a full-time job would have required unsustainable hours that burned out everyone who tried it. AI changed that equation entirely. It did not remove the effort required to build something meaningful—it removed the friction that used to make the effort impossible to sustain.

None of this is me telling you to go start a business. That is not the point at all. The point is that you are going to end up with extra time whether you plan for it or not, and you need somewhere real for it to go. A list of experiences you want to have. Skills you want to get serious about developing. Relationships you have been meaning to invest in but never had the bandwidth for. Habits you know would change your life if you could just find a consistent window to build them.

Without a deliberate plan for where that reclaimed time goes, it will default to whatever is loudest. More meetings that did not need to happen. More requests from people who learned that you always say yes. More invisible labor that nobody sees and nobody rewards. That is exactly why reduction has to be intentional from the very start.

The three-phase reduction system becomes powerful only when you put it up against something real in your own life and your own work. Agreeing with the idea of automation, delegation, and elimination is the easy part. Everybody nods along when they hear it described in theory. The hard part is sitting down with your actual calendar, your actual inbox, your actual revenue streams, and your actual commitments and asking yourself honestly which parts of your current life genuinely deserve to stay and which ones are just taking up space out of habit.

When you start running the framework against your real work instead of a hypothetical example, patterns show up fast. You start noticing where time is going toward things that feel familiar but do not create any impact. Responsibilities that genuinely require your judgment start separating themselves from the ones that are just left over from an earlier version of your career or your business that you never got around to letting go of.

This chapter is not here to introduce more tools. It is here to show you what it looks like when someone takes this framework and uses it as a filter against the messy, complicated reality of actual work and actual life.

Automate

The first phase of reduction is identifying the work that follows the same pattern every single time and letting a machine handle it so you never have to think about it again. This sounds obvious when you say it out loud, but most people resist it for a reason that has nothing to do with technology. The work feels like it belongs to them.

Answering customer questions feels like caring about the customer. Adjusting pricing feels like staying close to the business. Monitoring fulfillment feels like being responsible. Letting go of those tasks can feel like letting go of control, even when holding onto them is exactly what keeps you stuck.

You already know you are capable of doing this work because that was never the question and it never will be. The question that matters is whether the work genuinely needs you specifically, your judgment, your creativity, and the expertise you have spent years building, in order to be done well.

If it does not, and if the outcome looks roughly the same every single time regardless of who sits down to handle it, then keeping it on your plate is not a sign of dedication or responsibility. It is a misuse of the very thing that makes you most valuable to the people and the organization counting on you.

Customer Support That Runs Without You

At some point in any growing business, customer support turns into a quiet drain that nobody talks about but everyone on the team can feel weighing things down. The same questions show up day after day, things like shipping timelines, refund requests, login problems, and policy questions that are already answered somewhere in the documentation that nobody ever seems to read.

Each individual inquiry only takes a few minutes to handle, but when you multiply that across dozens or even hundreds of them landing every single week, the cost in human attention and energy becomes staggering in ways that do not show up on any report.

When automated support routing first went live in my own business, the resistance was immediate and came from the inside more than anywhere else. It felt impersonal, like handing off something that should have a human touch behind it. It felt risky, because what happens if the system gets something wrong and a real customer has a terrible experience as a result? What nobody expected, myself included, was how much better the experience got for the customer once the system was up and running.

Common questions that used to sit in a queue for hours waiting for someone to type out the same answer for the 40th time that week were now getting resolved instantly. The complicated situations that genuinely needed a thoughtful human response started getting routed to the right team member faster than before because those people were no longer buried under a mountain of routine inquiries that never should have reached them in the first place.

The way this works is straightforward. AI pulls from your existing knowledge base, the documentation and policies you have already written, and uses that information to respond to the questions it can handle on its own. For anything that needs a human touch, it drafts a response that your team can review and send in seconds instead of composing from scratch.

When a situation crosses into territory that requires real judgment, the system escalates it to the right person automatically. Zendesk AI handles this well if your business already runs on that platform, and the setup is less complicated than most people expect it to be.

The goal was never to take humans out of customer support entirely. The goal is to stop burning your team's attention and energy on work that does not require either one, so that when a customer shows up with a situation that genuinely calls for a thoughtful and personal response, there is actually someone available who has the bandwidth to give them one instead of someone who is already drained from typing out the same answer for the 70th time before lunch.

Products and Revenue Streams That Run in the Background

If you sell digital products, courses, templates, or any kind of subscription, you already know exactly how this plays out. The launch is exciting and the energy is high and sales start rolling in and everything feels like it is working exactly the way you planned.

Then the excitement fades and what gets left behind is a long, quiet stretch of operational maintenance that eats far more time than anyone anticipated when the product was first created. Pre-sale questions trickle in one at a time throughout the day, email sequences slowly drift out of date without anyone noticing until the metrics start slipping, and small fulfillment hiccups pop up just often enough to keep you checking on things when you should be focused on something else.

The revenue might be growing on paper, but so is the invisible mountain of work required to keep it all running smoothly behind the scenes.

This is where automation completely changes the math on what it takes to keep a product generating revenue. AI can draft and maintain your landing page copy, generate and refresh email sequences based on how your customers are engaging instead of what you guessed they would do 6 months ago, handle the repetitive pre-sale questions that come in every single week, and alert you only when something genuinely breaks instead of requiring you to hover nervously over every moving part wondering what is about to go wrong.

Connecting your distribution platform to an automation layer through a tool like n8n means the conditional logic, the notifications, and the follow-up sequences all run on their own without you having to touch them or even think about them on a daily basis.

The shift this creates goes well beyond just saving a few hours a week. It fundamentally changes your relationship with revenue from something you have to actively babysit every single day to something that operates more like infrastructure you built once and trust to do its job. You check on it periodically to make sure everything is performing the way it should. You make improvements when the data tells you something needs to change. The rest of the time it just runs, quietly doing what it was designed to do while your attention goes toward the work that actually needs your brain behind it.

Financial Decisions Based on Rules Instead of Gut Feelings

Most financial decisions in a growing business are reactive. Something feels off, so you pull up a dashboard. A number looks wrong, so you adjust pricing or shift budget. By the time you see the problem and respond to it, the damage has already been sitting there for days or weeks.

Automation brings structure to this by letting you define the rules when you are thinking clearly and then letting the system watch the numbers around the clock so you do not have to. If your refund rate climbs past the threshold you already decided was acceptable, the system flags it the moment it happens instead of waiting for you to stumble across it during a review three weeks later.

If customer acquisition cost starts drifting above what you determined is sustainable for the business, the adjustment kicks in automatically based on logic you already thought through and approved ahead of time. The guessing and the gut reactions get replaced by a set of decisions you made deliberately during a calm moment, and the system enforces those decisions 24 hours a day whether you are actively watching the dashboard or sound asleep at 2 in the morning.

Connecting your payment data through Stripe to an automation platform like n8n and layering AI analysis on top of it means you can spot meaningful trends and catch real deviations the moment they start forming, without having to manually pull reports every week or sit around waiting for a monthly review that is already outdated by the time someone finally gets around to putting it together.

Delegate

The second phase is harder than the first for most people, not because the work is complicated but because letting go of it requires trust. Delegation means accepting that someone else can handle something you have been doing yourself, and for a lot of high performers, that acceptance does not come naturally.

Here is what I have learned from watching hundreds of professionals work through this phase. The ones who struggle with delegation almost always share the same belief underneath it all. They think it will take longer to explain the task than it would to just do it themselves. That belief is true exactly once. The first time you explain it, yes, it takes longer. Every time after that, you never have to touch it again. The math favors delegation almost immediately, but the feeling of losing control makes it hard to see that in the moment.

Getting Administrative Work Off Your Plate

Small administrative tasks almost never feel like a problem on their own because each one is so quick and so minor that it barely registers as real work. Booking a flight, requesting a refund, managing a subscription renewal, following up with a vendor who stopped responding 3 days ago, all of it takes just a few minutes and all of it feels too small and too simple to bother explaining to someone else when you could just knock it out yourself and move on.

The issue is that nobody ever stops to add up what all of those tiny moments cost across a full week, and when you finally do the math, the number is almost always bigger than you expected.

When you add all of those small tasks together across a full month, what you are looking at is hours of your time going toward work that does not require your judgment, does not benefit from your creativity, and does not need your expertise in any way to get done properly. The only reason most people are still handling these things themselves is that the effort of setting up the handoff to someone else feels like it would take longer than just doing it, which is true exactly once and never again after that.

AI changes that equation by handling the setup work that always felt like the reason not to delegate in the first place. A quick voice note or a few bullet points describing what needs to happen is all it takes for the AI to turn your rough instructions into a structured email, a clean checklist, or a detailed set of steps that a virtual assistant or team member can pick up and run with without ever needing to come back to you for clarification.

Your involvement starts and ends with defining the outcome, which takes about 30 seconds, and from that point forward someone else handles every part of the execution while you move on to whatever actually needs your attention.

Using a tool like ChatGPT or Claude to handle the structuring side and pairing it with a task platform like Notion AI to give your assistant a clear workspace to operate from means the entire handoff process ends up taking less time than just doing the task yourself would have in the first place, which is the exact moment most people realize they should have started delegating a long time ago.

Turning Your Knowledge Into Systems Others Can Follow

If people keep coming to you with the same operational questions week after week, it means there is institutional knowledge living inside your head that has never been written down in a way other people can access. Every one of those interruptions feels quick, but collectively they fragment your focus and make it impossible to get into the kind of deep work that moves things forward.

Delegation at this level stops being about handing off individual tasks and starts being about building a system that lets the people around you make the same decision you would make without needing to pull you into it at all.

AI can take the policies and logic that have been living inside your head for years, all of those "if this happens then do that" rules you apply instinctively without even thinking about it anymore, and turn them into structured decision trees that a teammate or assistant can follow step by step on their own. Routine situations that used to land on your desk get resolved independently by someone following the path you already mapped out, and the edge cases that genuinely require your specific input still find their way to you while everything else gets handled without your involvement ever being necessary.

Eliminate

The third phase is the most powerful and the most uncomfortable. Automation keeps the work but removes the effort. Delegation keeps the work but removes you from it. Elimination asks whether the work should exist at all.

Most people skip this phase entirely because cutting things feels riskier than optimizing them. Saying no to a client feels confrontational. Dropping a marketing channel feels like giving up. Walking away from a recurring meeting feels like losing a seat at the table.

The discomfort is real, but so is the cost of carrying work that has long since stopped earning its place in your life.

Clients Who Cost More Than They Are Worth

Every business has them: the customers who create a wildly disproportionate amount of friction compared to what they pay. The ones generating excessive support tickets week after week, constantly escalating situations that should never require escalation, producing margins that turn negative the moment you account for how much time and energy they consume, and draining your team emotionally in ways that quietly bleed into how those same people show up for every other customer they interact with for the rest of the day.

The problem is that most people try to make this decision in a moment of frustration instead of from a place of clear data, which means one of two things happens. Either they react too aggressively during a bad week and make a call they might regret, or they never act at all because they cannot figure out how to separate how exhausted and annoyed they feel from what the numbers are telling them about the relationship.

AI takes the emotion out of that decision by letting the numbers speak for themselves. Ticket frequency, profitability per account, refund patterns, and escalation history all get surfaced in a way that shows you clearly and objectively which relationships are costing your business more than they will ever return in revenue or goodwill. Running this analysis across your entire customer base through a tool like Power BI with Copilot gives you something most people have never had when facing this kind of conversation, which is an objective foundation built on real data instead of a gut feeling that is impossible to defend when someone pushes back and asks you to justify the decision.

Channels That Look Busy But Produce Nothing

Marketing grows a lot faster than it ever shrinks. Someone adds a new social platform because everyone else seems to be there. A campaign type nobody has tried before gets tested because a competitor had success with it. A content format launches because it felt like a good idea in the moment.

Every one of them starts with good intentions, but hardly any of them ever get cut even when it becomes obvious they are not producing results. Before long, your team is stretched across a dozen different channels while the work that actually brings in money is coming from just two or three of them.

AI can look at lead generation, revenue contribution, engagement levels, and the time your team is investing across every channel you are active on and lay out in plain terms exactly where the return is real versus where the effort is being wasted on something that looks busy but produces almost nothing. Cutting a channel stops being an emotional or political decision that everyone argues about and becomes something you can point to with clear data behind it that nobody can reasonably push back on.

Running these comparisons through GA4 paired with AI analysis in ChatGPT takes minutes, not days, and gives you the clarity to stop spreading your team thin and start focusing their energy on the places where it actually turns into something worth measuring.

Commitments That Look Important But Are Not

Some of the most expensive commitments on your calendar are the ones that feel the most respectable and the hardest to question. Sitting on a committee that meets every other week, serving on an advisory board that sounds impressive when you mention it, showing up to recurring meetings that have been happening for so long nobody can remember why they were originally scheduled, and attending industry events that photograph well for a LinkedIn post but have never once led to a meaningful conversation or a real business decision.

The social cost of stepping away from any of these feels high, which is exactly why most people never do it even when they quietly suspect the time would be better spent elsewhere. AI can help by turning the invisible cost into something you can actually see and measure.

A calendar analytics tool like Reclaim.ai combined with AI summaries of what came out of each commitment over the past few months can show you in hard numbers how much of your time is going toward these obligations compared to how many real decisions got made, how many meaningful relationships got built, or how many revenue-generating moments resulted from showing up.

Once those numbers are sitting in front of you in black and white, the decision to let go becomes much easier to defend, both to yourself when the guilt creeps in and to anyone else who asks why you stopped attending.

An Offer List That Has Grown Beyond What Makes Sense

Products and services pile up inside a business the same way clutter piles up inside a house. Every single one was added for a good reason at the time it was created, and every single one still feels like it belongs when you look at it individually. Put them all together, though, and what you end up with is a level of operational complexity that quietly slows everything down and stretches your team's attention across so many different things that none of them get the focus they deserve.

AI can look at your revenue, your profit margins, and the time your team spends on everything you currently sell and show you which small handful of products or services are doing the heavy lifting for your entire business. That idea people always talk about where roughly 20 percent of what you sell brings in 80 percent of your money stops being something you nod along to in meetings and becomes something you can see in real numbers that make the decision feel clear instead of scary.

Pulling your sales data into ChatGPT or running it through a BI tool with Copilot takes minutes and gives you the confidence to cut the things that are not pulling their weight without lying awake at night wondering if you just got rid of something that mattered more than it looked like it did.

Being the Person Every Question Flows Through

If every problem in your organization eventually finds its way to your desk, it might feel like proof that you are the most important person in the building. In reality, though, it means your ability to grow and scale is completely stuck because nothing moves forward without you personally touching it, and somewhere along the way you stopped being the leader who creates capacity for the people around you and became the bottleneck that the entire team has learned to work around.

An AI-powered knowledge tool like Glean connected to your internal systems can pull up prior decisions, relevant documentation, and suggested next steps so that your team has what they need to resolve issues on their own instead of walking over to your desk or sending you a message every single time something comes up.

When escalations do happen, they happen on purpose because the situation genuinely requires your specific judgment, not out of habit or because asking you was simply the fastest and easiest path anyone could think of.

Believing You Have to Be in the Room

Physical presence has a way of disguising itself as importance, and it is one of the hardest habits to break because it feels so justified in the moment. Sitting in the room feels like staying informed. Having a seat at the table feels like having real influence over what gets decided.

Over time, though, showing up everywhere starts getting confused with contributing something meaningful, and before you know it the calendar is packed with meetings that exist primarily so you can find out what happened rather than because you genuinely needed to be part of making it happen.

AI breaks this pattern completely by making it possible to stay fully informed about everything that happens in a meeting without ever needing to physically be there. A tool like Fathom can record, summarize, and organize everything that gets said so that nothing gets lost whether you were sitting in the room or halfway across the country doing something that needed your attention.

Giving up an hour of your day just to sit through a conversation you could absorb in 5 minutes by reading a clear summary stops making any kind of sense once you have experienced the alternative. Pairing that with a search tool like Glean that pulls together decisions and context from across every platform your team uses means that catching up on what was discussed, what was decided, and what still needs attention becomes something you can do from anywhere and at any time in a tiny fraction of the time it would have taken to attend the meeting yourself.

Reduction is what creates the space that makes everything else in this book possible. It is what gives you room to experiment with new ideas without burning yourself out in the process, and it is what lets you move through your work with real intention instead of constantly reacting to whatever happens to land in front of you next.

In a world where AI keeps compressing how long it takes to execute the work on your plate, the people who come out ahead are not just the ones who get good at cutting things out of their schedule. They are the ones who take the space that opens up and use it to build something new, learn something they did not know before, adjust when the first attempt does not go the way they hoped, and then build again with everything they picked up along the way.

Before moving to the next chapter, open your calendar for the coming week and look at every single commitment sitting on it. For each one, ask yourself whether it should be automated, delegated, or eliminated entirely. Mark at least three items that you know in your gut do not deserve the time they are currently taking from you.

Acting on all of them right away is not the point. Seeing them clearly for what they are is what matters right now, and once you can see them you will not be able to unsee them. The scoring worksheet to help you work through this process is available at `http://myaiworkweek.com/reduction`.

The next chapter is about building the muscle that makes everything you have learned so far stick for good. Not waiting around until every detail is perfect before you take the first step. Not hiding behind preparation and planning as an excuse to avoid putting something real out into the world where people can actually see it.

It is about learning how to build something in public while you are still working a full-time job, how to test ideas and put them in front of real people while you are still figuring out what works, and how to ship work that genuinely matters while you are still in the middle of becoming the kind of person who does this for a living.

Perfectionist's Paradox

The biggest trap in AI adoption is not fear of change, and it is not a lack of budget or technical skills either. It is perfectionism disguising itself as quality control, and it is everywhere once you start looking for it.

Teams spend 3 months "researching" the perfect AI tool when they could have tested one in 3 days and learned more from that single experiment than any comparison spreadsheet would ever tell them.

Leaders demand 99 percent accuracy before they are willing to implement anything at all, then sit around wondering why their competitors are moving faster and getting results they have not even started chasing yet. People build elaborate workflows on paper and in slide decks that look impressive in a planning meeting but never actually press the start button because something about it still does not feel quite ready.

Perfectionism does not protect quality. It kills momentum, and it turns AI from something that could be accelerating your entire organization into just another excuse for why nothing has changed yet.

What makes perfectionism so seductive in the AI era is that it sounds responsible when you say it out loud. It disguises itself as risk management, and nobody questions it because the language is so reasonable. Leaders tell themselves they are protecting their teams from unnecessary disruption, protecting customers from a bad experience, and protecting the company from public embarrassment.

All of that sounds smart and measured until you look underneath it and realize something more personal is driving the hesitation. AI exposes competence in a way that feels very visible and very public. When an automation you built fails in front of other people, it does not just feel like a technical glitch. It feels like your judgment failed.

When a workflow you designed breaks down, it does not just feel like a process issue. It feels like your credibility is breaking down right along with it. The instinct to over plan and over prepare before launching anything is almost always an instinct to protect your identity from that kind of exposure, and the longer that instinct goes unexamined and unchallenged, the longer real implementation sits on the shelf collecting dust while everyone around you moves forward.

The paradox at the center of all this is painfully simple. The pursuit of a perfect AI implementation is the very thing that prevents most people and most organizations from ever implementing AI at all. While you are still planning and testing and going back to the drawing board to plan some more, your competition is already shipping real work, learning from what breaks, and making it better with every single iteration.

The reason they are pulling ahead has nothing to do with having flawless systems. It has everything to do with the fact that their systems exist in the real world doing real work while yours is still sitting inside a slide deck waiting for someone to feel confident enough to hit go.

I learned this the hard way during my first major AI project rollout. We were implementing automated customer onboarding for a client that was bringing in over 500 new customers every single month. The manual process was eating roughly 40 hours of staff time every week, and the error rate kept climbing right alongside the volume in a way that made it clear something had to change before the whole thing fell apart.

Instead of starting small and building from there, we tried to design the perfect system right out of the gate. Every possible customer scenario got mapped out in detail. Conditional logic got built for edge cases that realistically only happened once or twice a year. Historical data going back two full years got run through the system to make sure nothing had been missed. Six weeks later, what we had was a beautiful and impressively complex automation that could theoretically handle absolutely anything thrown at it.

The first time a customer uploaded a file format that nobody had thought to plan for, the entire system crashed. Instead of automatically processing 90 percent of customers and having a human step in to handle the remaining 10 percent, we were right back to processing 100 percent of them manually while the team scrambled to figure out what went wrong with the automation we had spent 6 weeks building.

That failure taught me something I have never forgotten. Chasing perfection is what keeps things from ever getting finished, and refusing to ship something until it is finished is what keeps it from ever existing in the first place. The smarter approach, the one I use now on every single project, would have been to start with the 80 percent use case and nothing more.

Build an automation that handled the most common customer type flawlessly and let a real person catch everything else. Get it launched in 2 weeks instead of 6. Learn from how real customers used the system instead of running endless theoretical tests in a vacuum. Make improvements based on the things that broke in production instead of the things someone imagined might break during a planning session.

When we finally rebuilt the system with that mindset, we had it live in 8 days. It handled 85 percent of onboarding automatically from day one. The remaining 15 percent flowed to a simple manual queue. Within 2 weeks of real-world use, we identified the next automation opportunity and added it. By week 4, we were at 92 percent automated. The difference between the first attempt and the second was not technical skill. It was philosophy. We stopped chasing perfection and started chasing progress.

Here is the truth about AI implementation that most people do not want to hear. You will never know enough to build the perfect system on your first try, no matter how much research you do or how many planning sessions you sit through before launching. The data you need to make the system great only shows up after the system is live and real people are using it in ways you did not predict.

Customer behavior surprises you in directions nobody in the room thought to plan for. Edge cases that never came up in testing reveal themselves the moment real volume starts flowing through. New tools hit the market that make your original approach feel outdated before you even finished rolling it out. Waiting for perfect clarity before you are willing to start is a trap that guarantees you will always be starting and never be learning.

There is also a compounding learning gap that perfectionists drastically underestimate. The team that launches today, even with something rough and incomplete, begins building real insight immediately. How users behave becomes visible instead of something everyone guesses at in a conference room. Which features people care about and which ones nobody touches becomes obvious within the first few weeks.

Prompts, logic, and guardrails start getting refined based on friction that actually happened instead of friction someone imagined might happen during a planning session. Every single week of iteration sharpens the team's instincts in ways that no amount of prelaunch preparation could ever replicate.

Meanwhile, the team still sitting in the planning phase is not standing still. It is actively falling behind in the kind of knowledge that only comes from getting your hands dirty with a live system. When it comes to AI, the intuition that gets built through real-world use becomes a genuine competitive advantage over time, and that kind of intuition cannot be picked up from a whitepaper or a webinar. It has to be earned through messy, imperfect cycles of shipping something, watching what happens, and making it better the next time around.

The companies winning with AI right now are not the ones running flawless systems that never break. They are the ones comfortable enough to ship version 0.8 knowing it is not perfect and then improve it a little bit every single week based on what they learn from real usage. Having a working automation that saves 20 hours a week starting today will always beat a theoretical one that might save 30 hours a week if it ever gets finished 6 months from now. When the entire game is about learning faster than everyone else, speed beats perfection every single time.

If you find yourself stuck in planning mode unable to pull the trigger on anything, there is one question that can break the cycle. What is the smallest version of this that could go live this week? Not the best version. Not the complete version. Not the version you would be proud to show off at a conference.

The smallest functional version that creates measurable value for a real person doing real work: Build that version and nothing more. Put it into the world. Watch what breaks and pay close attention to what surprises you. Fix the things that need fixing. Then do the whole thing again with everything you just learned, and keep doing it until the system is something you never could have designed from a planning document alone.

I worked with a marketing team that spent four full months planning their AI content calendar system before a single piece of it went live. Every possible content type was mapped out in detail. Every approval workflow was documented from start to finish. Every edge case for holidays, product launches, and seasonal campaigns was accounted for and built into the logic. Mockups were created, stakeholder reviews were scheduled and held, and thorough documentation was written for a system that did not actually exist yet in any functional form.

When they finally launched it after all of that preparation, the system worked for exactly 3 days before everything started falling apart.

A new product announcement hit and everything they had built became irrelevant overnight. The carefully planned workflows were suddenly obsolete. The content types that had been mapped out so thoroughly no longer matched what the team needed to produce. The approval structure that looked so clean on paper did not reflect how anyone on the team was working anymore. Four months of meticulous planning collapsed under 72 hours of contact with reality.

Compare that to another team I worked with that took a completely different approach. Instead of trying to build the perfect system before launching anything, they spent 2 days putting together a basic AI content calendar that handled their three most common content types and nothing else. It was rough around the edges, it had bugs that needed fixing, and the interface was clunky in ways that would have made the first team cringe. But it worked well enough to use, so they launched it on a Monday and ran their entire week through it.

What they learned in those 7 days about how their team creates and manages content was more valuable than anything the first team picked up across 4 months of theoretical planning. Features they assumed would be critical turned out to be things nobody used. Workflows they never anticipated emerged naturally once real people started interacting with the system every day. Automation opportunities that would have been completely invisible inside a planning document became obvious the moment real work started flowing through it.

Within 6 weeks, that scrappy version 0.8 that nobody would have been proud to demo on day one had evolved into a system that outperformed everything the first team spent months designing on paper. The second team was not smarter and did not have access to better tools or a bigger budget. They simply started learning 4 months earlier than the team that was still trying to get everything perfect before they would allow themselves to begin.

That is the real cost of perfectionism that nobody talks about. It is not just the time you waste sitting in planning mode. It is all of the learning you never get to do while your competitors are out in the real world iterating, improving, and pulling further ahead with every passing week.

The best AI implementations I have seen across every industry and every team size all follow the same pattern. They start small, ship fast, learn from what happens constantly, and improve with every single cycle without ever treating any version as the final one. Every release is assumed to be temporary and every assumption is expected to be wrong about something, which is why feedback loops get built in from the very beginning to catch problems quickly instead of letting them quietly pile up in the background.

Perfectionism creates another problem on top of all of that, one that is harder to see but just as damaging. It raises the stakes so impossibly high that any failure starts to feel catastrophic instead of normal. When you pour months of work into building what was supposed to be the "perfect" system, every flaw that surfaces after launch stops feeling like a natural part of the process and starts feeling like proof that all of that time and effort was wasted. That fear of failure makes you even more conservative the next time around, which slows everything down even further and feeds the exact cycle that caused the problem in the first place.

Iteration is what lowers the stakes to a level where experimentation feels possible. If you ship something small in a week and it completely falls flat, you lost a week. That is recoverable. You look at what went wrong, adjust your approach, rebuild it, and try again with everything you just learned. The cost of failure stays low enough that taking risks and testing ideas stops feeling dangerous and starts feeling like the smartest way to spend your time.

Perfectionism Is Just Fear With a Better Résumé

One client told me she had been "planning to implement AI" for over a year. Every single time we talked, there was a new reason to wait just a little bit longer. More tools needed to be researched before she could make a decision. Another conference was coming up that might give her the clarity she was looking for. A big project was wrapping up soon and once it was done her team would finally have the bandwidth to focus on something new. There was always one more thing standing between her and actually starting.

I finally asked her a question that was more blunt than anything I had said to her before. What are you afraid will happen if you start today with something imperfect? She went quiet for a long moment and then admitted the thing she had never said out loud to anyone. She was terrified of looking incompetent in front of her own team.

The image she kept playing in her head was launching an AI tool that failed publicly, and watching her team lose confidence in her judgment as a result. That single fear had kept her completely paralyzed for 12 straight months while the world moved forward without her.

We reframed the entire conversation around the smallest possible starting point. Instead of launching some big AI initiative that would put her reputation on the line, we picked one tiny experiment that nobody would even notice unless it worked. She would use AI to draft the agenda for her weekly team meeting. That was it. No announcement, no fanfare, no pressure, and no audience watching to see if she succeeded or failed.

She started the following week. The first agenda the AI drafted was mediocre at best, and she ended up editing it heavily before sending it out. The second one came back noticeably better and needed less reworking. By the third week she was barely touching the drafts at all before they went out to her team. Within a month she had saved 10 hours of her time and more importantly she had proven to herself that an imperfect AI tool could still deliver real, measurable value without the catastrophic failure she had been imagining for an entire year.

That one small win gave her the confidence to try something bigger, and then something bigger after that. Six months later she had automated five major workflows across her team and saved over 200 hours that were now going toward work that needed human thinking behind it. None of it would have happened if she had kept waiting for the perfect plan to reveal itself, because that plan was never going to arrive on its own. It only became visible after she started moving.

The mistake perfectionists make over and over again is confusing "good enough to start" with "not good enough at all," as if those two things are the same when they could not be more different. Good enough to start means you understand the problem, you have a solution that could plausibly work, and you have a way to measure whether it made things better. That is the bar, and it is a much lower bar than most people are willing to accept. Anything beyond that level of preparation before you launch is not diligence. It is stalling dressed up in responsible sounding language.

The Three Checks

Here is the framework I use every single time I need to decide whether it is time to stop planning and start building. I call it the Three Checks, and it has saved me from my own perfectionist tendencies more times than I can count.

The first check is whether I can explain the problem I am trying to solve in two sentences or less. If I can do that clearly and simply, it means I understand the problem well enough to start working on it. If I cannot, it usually means I need to think more, not plan more.

The second check is whether I have a solution that could realistically work, even if it is not the most elegant or optimized version of that solution. If something plausible is sitting in front of me that has a reasonable chance of improving the situation, that is enough to move forward with.

The third check is whether I have a way to measure if the solution made things better once it is live. If I can look at real numbers or real feedback and tell whether the change moved things in the right direction, then I have everything I need to learn and iterate from the moment it launches.

If all three of those boxes get checked, planning stops and building begins. Everything else, every optimization and every additional layer of polish, is refinement that can happen after the thing is out in the world doing real work. This does not mean risks get ignored or that launching recklessly is somehow a good idea. It means accepting that some risks can only be understood by encountering them, not by theorizing about them in a meeting room.

You cannot plan your way around every possible problem no matter how hard you try. At some point, assumptions have to be tested against reality, and the only way to do that is to put something real in front of real people and see what happens.

Build It Ugly, Fix It Later

One of my favorite examples of this came from a financial services client who wanted to automate their monthly reporting process. The manual version of that process was eating 12 hours of staff time every single month, and the volume and complexity were only going to keep growing. The perfectionist approach would have been to sit down and map every single report, every data source, and every formatting requirement across the entire organization before anyone was allowed to build anything. Instead, we picked the single most time-consuming report out of the whole batch and automated just that one by itself.

It took 3 days to build and it saved 4 hours a month right out of the gate. It was not perfect by any stretch. There were formatting inconsistencies that would have made a perfectionist lose sleep. The data refresh still had to be triggered manually instead of running on its own. But it worked well enough to deliver real value from day one, and that was all that mattered at that stage.

That first win did more than just prove the concept was viable. It revealed things about the process that we never could have discovered from inside a planning document no matter how thorough it was. Two of the data sources turned out to be unreliable in ways that only became visible once real data was flowing through the automation, which meant they needed cleaning before anything else could be built on top of them.

One particular report format turned out to matter far more to the stakeholders than anyone on the team had realized, which completely changed the priority order for the rest of the project. The team itself made something clear through how they used the system that nobody had thought to ask about ahead of time, which was that they cared significantly more about getting their reports faster than they cared about every detail being formatted perfectly.

Armed with everything we learned from that first imperfect launch, the second report got automated in 2 days instead of 3. The third one took a single day. By the time we reached the 10th report, the whole process had been refined so many times through real use that what used to take days was happening in hours. The entire project from start to finish took 6 weeks and saved 120 hours a year of work that no human ever needed to be doing in the first place.

A perfectionist approach to that same project would still be sitting in the planning phase right now, waiting for someone to feel ready enough to begin.

Perfect systems do not exist anywhere in the real world, but working systems do, and a working system that gets a little bit better every single week will always outperform a perfect system that never makes it off the whiteboard. If you take one thing away from this entire chapter and carry it with you into every AI project you ever touch, let it be this. Your first version is going to be bad, and that is not failure.

That is the entry price for learning something that can only be learned by doing it. The faster you are willing to pay that price, the faster real improvement begins. The longer you sit on the sidelines waiting to feel ready, the further behind you fall while everyone willing to be messy keeps pulling ahead.

Right now, before you turn to the next chapter, give yourself what I call the 48-hour challenge. Pick one task you have been meaning to automate but keep putting off because the timing never feels quite right. Set a hard deadline of 48 hours from this exact moment. Build something that works well enough to use, not something that is polished enough to present.

Put it into action and watch what happens. Pay attention to what breaks and what surprises you. Then fix what needs to be fixed next week and make it better the week after that. The point is not to get it right on the first try but to finally get it started.

Chapter 5

Maximize Efficiency Gains

At this point, you are probably feeling like things are moving at a good pace and that the hard part might already be behind you. A few automations are actually working the way they are supposed to. Time is showing back up on calendars that used to be completely packed. Inboxes are quieter than they have been in months, and follow-ups are getting cleaner without anyone having to chase them down. It feels like real momentum, and it feels earned—because it is.

This is usually the exact moment when people tell themselves to keep pushing forward because clearly this whole AI thing is working and the results are only going to keep getting better from here. This is also the exact moment when most people walk straight off a cliff they never saw coming, something I call the drop-off zone.

The drop-off zone is what happens right after your first real efficiency win, and almost nobody sees it coming because it disguises itself as progress. You find what feels like magic automation beans and suddenly every tool you come across promises to give you and your team even more time back than the last one did.

One promises to fix your meetings for good. Another claims it can completely rewrite your entire sales process from the ground up. A third one swears it will eliminate follow-ups forever so that nobody on your team ever has to chase anyone down again. You start grabbing them one after another because each one sounds just reasonable enough to justify, and because the pain of being overwhelmed and buried in busywork is still fresh enough in your body that anything promising relief feels worth trying.

A few weeks later, you're staring at a credit card statement and realizing you're now spending $300 a month on AI subscriptions. Your team has logins for tools they barely remember signing up for. People are asking which system is the source of truth. Work is moving faster in theory but messier in practice. You didn't lose control because AI failed. You lost control because you mistook speed for coordination.

AI can increase efficiency inside a single team almost overnight. One group automates their reporting, another streamlines their email workflows, and a third accelerates how fast they produce content, all within a matter of days. The problem is that local efficiency inside one team does not automatically translate into things working well across the entire organization.

Without someone intentionally paying attention to the bigger picture, multiple teams start adopting tools that overlap with each other without anyone realizing it. Data starts flowing through parallel systems that were never designed to talk to one another. Different departments build automations that solve the exact same problem in slightly different ways using completely different logic.

The organization ends up moving faster at the edges where individual teams are seeing real wins, while quietly becoming more fragmented and harder to coordinate at the center where everything is supposed to come together.

This is the part that nobody warns you about when you are celebrating those early wins. The efficiency gains that feel so real and so earned create a false sense of confidence that everything is on the right track, and that false confidence is what leads directly to tool sprawl.

Without a deliberate system holding everything together, AI does not actually simplify how work gets done. It multiplies the complexity in ways that are almost impossible to notice while they are happening. You do not feel it right away, which is exactly what makes the drop-off zone so dangerous. By the time the problems become visible enough for someone to raise a flag, you are already paying for them in wasted money, scattered attention, and eroded trust from a team that was excited about AI 3 months ago and is now quietly wondering whether any of it was worth the trouble.

Trust erosion is the most dangerous cost of tool sprawl, and it is the hardest one to reverse once it takes hold. When the people on your team are not sure which automation is the one they should actually trust, they stop trusting all of them and go back to doing things manually the way they always did before.

When two dashboards show different numbers for the same metric, people quietly close both of them and open the old spreadsheet they have been keeping on the side just in case. When outputs from different tools contradict each other or feel inconsistent, confidence in the entire system drops to a level where getting people to engage with any of it becomes an uphill battle.

Once that trust is gone, adoption slows to a crawl and the problem stops being a technical one that can be fixed with better configuration. It becomes a cultural one that can only be fixed by simplifying the stack, making it crystal clear who owns what, and enforcing consistency across every tool and every workflow until people start believing in the system again.

I know this because I have lived through it personally, and I have watched clients repeat the same pattern almost step for step like they were following a script nobody handed them. That is why this chapter exists in the first place. The goal here is not to pile more AI on top of what you have already built. It is to keep you from accidentally re-creating the same chaos you were trying to escape, just wrapped in shinier software with a monthly subscription attached.

If you pay close attention to what comes next, you can avoid the drop-off zone entirely and move into the part where efficiency actually sticks around long enough to change how your organization works for good.

The leaders who actually hold on to their efficiency gains over time understand that governance matters just as much as innovation. Every tool has one person who owns it and is accountable for whether it is delivering value or just taking up space. Every data stream has a single source of truth that everyone agrees on so there is never a question about which number is the right one.

Regular audits happen to catch and eliminate systems that have become redundant before they have a chance to create confusion. New tools do not get added unless someone can point to a clear use case that justifies bringing them in, and even then the bar is high enough that most requests get turned down. The AI stack gets treated like a portfolio that needs regular pruning to stay healthy, not like a collection that is supposed to keep growing forever.

If you are reading this and starting to suspect that your organization might already be drifting into the drop-off zone, there are a few signals that will tell you for sure. Your subscription count is climbing faster than any measurable outcome can justify. Multiple tools across different teams claim to solve the same workflow but do it in completely different ways.

Team members have started asking where information "really lives" because they have lost confidence that any single source has the full picture. Nobody on the team can clearly explain why a specific tool was chosen over any of the alternatives or what problem it was originally brought in to solve.

When those signals start showing up, the smartest thing you can do is stop expanding immediately and shift all of that energy toward integrating and simplifying what you already have before adding anything else to the pile.

Productivity at a New Baseline

By now you understand the trap that comes with early wins and you know what the drop-off zone looks like before it hits. The question this chapter answers is what comes after you avoid it. Because once the obvious automations are running and the initial time savings are real, most teams hit a wall they did not expect.

Individual departments are moving faster than ever, but the organization as a whole starts to feel like a collection of fast-moving parts that were never designed to work together. That disconnect between speed inside a team and clarity across the company is where the real work of AI leadership begins.

When AI speeds up how fast work gets done, it has a way of showing you all the cracks that were a lot easier to ignore when everything moved slowly enough to cover them up. Marketing suddenly bringing in leads twice as fast sounds great until you realize the sales team still cannot agree on what a good lead looks like, which means the tension between those two groups does not get better with speed—it gets a whole lot worse.

Product shipping new features faster than ever sounds like progress until you notice that nobody built a real way for customer feedback to make it back to the people deciding what to build next, which means the gap between what customers want and what they are getting grows faster than anyone expected.

Tools that can summarize entire meetings in seconds sound like a dream until it turns out that different teams are using the same words to mean completely different things, which just means everyone can now misunderstand each other at twice the speed they used to.

This is the point where productivity stops being about how fast any single team can move and starts being about whether the whole company was ever set up to handle the pace it just created.

As AI tools spread across every department and embed themselves into the platforms people use every single day, the thing holding most organizations back changes in a way that catches leadership off guard. The bottleneck is no longer about how much work teams can produce because AI has already solved that problem for most of them. The bottleneck becomes whether all of that output is pointed in the same direction, and for most companies the honest answer is that it is not.

That realization is why some of the largest companies in the world are quietly reorganizing how their teams are structured. More and more organizations are pulling marketing, sales, and customer success under a single revenue leader who can see the full picture instead of letting each group optimize in isolation.

In some cases, even product is being folded into that same structure so that what gets built and what gets sold and what gets supported are all being guided by the same set of priorities. This is not the kind of cosmetic restructuring that happens when a new executive wants to put their stamp on the org chart. It is a direct response to the reality that when every team has powerful AI tools accelerating their work independently, optimizing inside silos is no longer just inefficient—it is genuinely dangerous.

When every department is running its own stack of tools, following its own automation logic, and measuring success against its own unique definition of what winning looks like, AI does not bring those groups closer together. It amplifies the disagreements between them and makes the disconnects louder and more visible than they have ever been.

Too many tools pulling data in different directions. Too many dashboards showing different versions of the same story. Too many interpretations of what the numbers mean floating around the same conference room. Too many people spending their time negotiating with each other over things that a well-designed system should be handling automatically.

The companies that are actually redefining what productivity means right now are not sitting around asking how to make individual departments move faster. They are asking a fundamentally different question, which is how to reduce the friction that builds up across the entire journey a customer takes from the first time they hear about the company to the moment they decide to stay or leave.

Before you can get anywhere near that kind of thinking, though, there is an uncomfortable question that needs to be asked honestly and answered without defensiveness: Are you married to your tech stack?

The Tech Stack Marriage Audit

Most organizations inherit their stack rather than design it. A leader selects a core platform during the growth phase. Another team adds a project system to solve a short-term problem. A communication tool becomes standard because it was convenient. Over time, these decisions harden into infrastructure. Questioning them feels disruptive, even disloyal.

Tools are not partners you owe loyalty to. They are instruments that either serve what you are trying to accomplish right now or they do not, and holding on to one because of how much time or money went into setting it up 2 years ago is not strategy. It is sentimentality with a subscription fee attached. Run this audit honestly and be willing to hear what the answers tell you even if they are uncomfortable.

Who Is in Charge?

Start simple: Does every important system have one clear owner, or does everyone just use whatever they're used to? Do all your teams agree on what words like "qualified lead" or "active customer" actually mean? Are your shared numbers built into your systems automatically, or do people argue about them in meetings every week?

If your definitions only exist in PowerPoint slides instead of your actual workflows, things will break.

Are You Using the Same Tool Twice?

Are multiple systems tracking the same information? Do different teams use different dashboards to look at what should be the same number? Did people build the same automation in two different places just because nobody checked what already existed? Having backups feels safe when you're small, but when you grow it just creates confusion.

Are You Actually Using Your AI Features?

Are the AI tools you already own turned on, or are they just sitting there unused? Has anyone trained your team to use those features on purpose, or is everyone just using default settings? Is your AI helping different teams work together, or is each department only using it for their own stuff? Turning on AI in one department isn't the same as redesigning how your whole company works.

Can You See the Whole Picture?

Test your visibility. Can someone follow a customer's entire journey from first website visit to renewal without jumping between totally different systems? When one team hands work to another team, does the system make it happen automatically, or does it only work if someone remembers to do it?

When a customer might leave, do the right teams find out on their own without anyone having to tell them? If you can't see the whole customer journey, you can't fix the whole customer journey.

Are Your Tools Worth What They Cost?

Finally, check the money. Does each major tool connect to a clear business result? Are your software bills growing faster than your actual improvements? When is the last time you deleted a tool instead of adding one? Piling up more tools without a clear plan isn't progress—it's just clutter.

If these questions are hard to answer, the problem isn't that your team isn't working hard enough–the problem is how everything is set up. When I look at most companies' software, I don't see one organized system. I see four separate towers that don't talk to each other.

Four Separate Layers

Each department has built its own set of tools. They picked what works best for their own goals and added software based on their own needs. When AI came along, most companies added it inside each tower separately. This made individual departments faster at their own work, but it did not actually connect the towers to each other or help them work together better.

Before we talk about how to connect departments, we need to understand what we are working with. Every department's technology can be broken down into three distinct layers that build on each other. Inside each of those layers, the tools can exist in three different stages of sophistication.

The first stage is traditional tools that require manual work. The second stage is AI turned on, where the tools get smarter and can surface insights automatically. The third stage is AI plus automation working together, where insights do not just appear but actually trigger actions across systems without anyone needing to manually move information around.

Most companies today are somewhere between the first two stages. They have traditional tools and maybe some AI features turned on. Very few companies operate in the third stage, where AI and automation work together seamlessly across their entire stack.

Now we will examine what these three layers actually look like in practice. We will walk through the marketing department first, then the sales department, and finally the customer experience department. This will help you see where your own organization sits and what the path forward looks like.

The Marketing Tech Stack

Every tech stack has four layers that build on each other. Most companies have added AI features within each layer, making individual tools smarter. But very few have redesigned how those layers work together. Table 5.1 shows what each layer does and how it evolves from traditional tools to full integration.

You can tell when you are moving from AI as a shiny feature in your tech stack to having a truly connected system by looking at what problems get solved without you touching them. If AI is just making your individual tools faster or smarter, you are still in the second column. But when your system starts proactively solving cross-functional problems that you used to handle manually, like automatically stopping ads to new customers or updating messaging when sales stages change, that is when you know you are building something actually integrated.

The Sales Tech Stack

Sales is where intent turns into revenue. Marketing might generate demand and create awareness, but sales is the function that converts opportunity into actual commitment. If the marketing stack is about

Table 5.1 The four tech stack layers

Layer	The job	Basic setup	AI features turned on	Actually connected
Data & Identity	Which person opened your emails, visited your website, downloaded your content, and how all those actions connect to one contact record	You use a CRM (customer relationship management) system like Salesforce or HubSpot to collect prospect information like names and emails and update those records manually. If you have duplicate contact records in your CRM system, you have a basic setup.	Your CRM system automatically figures out when duplicate records are the same person and merges them. It also predicts which leads are most likely to buy.	When you learn something about a customer anywhere in your system, that information updates everywhere else instantly.

(continued)

Table 5.1 Continued

Layer	The job	Basic setup	AI features turned on	Actually connected
Intelligence & Decision-Making	Which contacts qualify for which campaigns based on their actions, job role, company size, or engagement level	You manually create email lists in tools like HubSpot or Salesforce based on job titles or company size. When you want to change who gets targeted, you update the list yourself.	Your email lists rebuild themselves automatically when people take actions. The tool suggests which automations you should set up next.	When your sales team notices certain types of leads never close, your marketing system stops targeting those people without you changing anything.
Communication Tools	The actual emails, text messages, and automated sequences that get sent to contacts	You use tools like HubSpot, Marketo, or Klaviyo to write email campaigns and schedule them to send at specific times to specific lists you picked.	The tool writes subject line options for you, picks the best send time, and changes what happens next based on whether people click or ignore the email.	When someone becomes a paying customer in your sales system, every marketing email instantly adjusts to match that, and they get added to customer-only messages automatically.

Where Customers See You	The ads they see on social media, what your website shows them, and conversations in chat widgets	You set up ads in Facebook, Google, and LinkedIn, pick your audience, and manually adjust your budget when you check performance.	Facebook and Google automatically adjust how much to bid and who to show ads to based on who's clicking.	When someone becomes a customer, all your ads stop showing to them immediately across every platform without you turning anything off.

identifying and nurturing prospects, the sales stack is about turning those prospects into paying customers.

The structure looks different, but the architectural challenge is exactly the same, as shown in Table 5.2. Tools accumulate over time. AI features get layered in. Individual efficiency improves. But cross-functional flow remains broken unless you deliberately redesign it.

You can tell when you are moving from AI as a helpful feature to having a truly connected system by watching what problems get solved without you doing anything. If AI is just helping salespeople write better emails or showing managers which deals might be at risk, you are still in the second column. But when your system starts proactively solving problems across teams, like automatically updating marketing based on what sales learns or alerting customer success when deals progress, that is when you know you are building something actually integrated.

The Customer Experience Tech Stack

Once a deal closes, the relationship changes completely. You move from trying to win the customer to trying to keep them. Customer experience teams pick up where sales left off, and their entire job is to deliver on whatever was promised during the sales process. That means onboarding new accounts, handling support requests, tracking how much the product is actually being used, collecting feedback, and keeping a close eye on whether accounts are healthy or heading toward the exit.

For years, most of this work has been reactive. Someone submits a ticket, and the team responds. A complaint comes in, and someone addresses it. A customer success manager schedules a check-in call, reviews the notes, and hopes to catch warning signs before a customer decides to leave.

Table 5.2 The sales tech stack layers

Layer	What this layer controls	Basic setup	AI features turned on	Actually connected
CRM & System of Record	Every customer account, contact person, sales opportunity, what stage each deal is in, and revenue forecasts	You use Salesforce or Pipedrive to track accounts and deals. Sales reps manually move deals from one stage to the next like "qualified lead" to "proposal sent" to "closed won." Forecasting relies on what reps tell their managers. The system tracks everything but depends on people remembering to update it.	Salesforce Einstein predicts which deals will close and flags opportunities that might fall through. HubSpot surfaces how engaged each contact is automatically. Forecasting uses models instead of just guessing. The system captures activity automatically by syncing with email and calendars.	When the system predicts a deal will close, it automatically updates marketing's rules about who qualifies as a good lead. When a deal moves to the next stage, it triggers preparation for onboarding and alerts the customer success team without anyone sending an email. Revenue warnings inform the product team without manual reporting.

(continued)

Table 5.2 Continued

Layer	What this layer controls	Basic setup	AI features turned on	Actually connected
Data & Intelligence	Contact information like phone numbers and emails, company details like size and industry, signals that show buying intent, and which accounts to prioritize	You use tools like ZoomInfo, Apollo, or Clay to get phone numbers, emails, and company information. Reps manually add this information to accounts and decide on their own which prospects look promising. Intent data might get reviewed sometimes but mostly stays static.	Signals that show someone is researching your type of product feed automatically into your CRM. Scoring that combines company fit and behavior determines routing. The platform tells you which accounts you should focus on next based on data.	Account scores influence not just who gets routed to which rep, but also what messages get sent.

Engagement & Conversation	Email sequences to prospects, phone calls, meeting scheduling, and recordings of every sales conversation	You use platforms like Outreach, Salesloft, or Apollo to manage email and call sequences. Calendly schedules meetings. Tools like Gong or Zoom IQ record and transcribe calls. Reps run multistep outreach campaigns and managers listen to call recordings to coach.	The platform writes email drafts for you, picks the best time to send, and recommends what to do next. Gong analyzes conversations, spots risks, and automatically adds structured notes to the CRM. AI points out objections, when competitors get mentioned, and whether the prospect sounds positive or negative.	Insights from conversations automatically update customer profiles that marketing and customer success use. When prospects keep bringing up the same objection, marketing campaigns get updated to address it. When certain types of deals keep falling through, the product team gets alerted to review why. When deal sentiment changes, forecasts and messaging update across the company.

(continued)

Table 5.2 Continued

Layer	What this layer controls	Basic setup	AI features turned on	Actually connected
Sales Content & Buyer Experience	Content libraries with case studies and pitch decks, interactive product demos, digital sales rooms where buyers can review materials, and everything prospects see during the buying process	You use platforms like Highspot, Seismic, or Showpad to store sales content and playbooks. Demo tools like Walnut or Navattic let prospects explore the product. Reps use these to stay consistent in what they show and say.	The platform recommends which content to share based on what stage the deal is in. Tools surface what action to take next and which deals might be at risk. Demos personalize themselves based on who is watching.	How buyers use content feeds directly into updates for marketing messaging. Data on buyer engagement influences automated messages after someone becomes a customer. Warnings from the revenue system inform what features the product team should prioritize and how to prevent cancellations. How engaged someone is in a sales room adjusts account-based marketing targeting automatically.

The data that could help predict these problems usually lives in too many different places and moves too slowly between teams. By the time something shows up as a red flag in one system, the customer has already started making decisions somewhere else.

AI has started changing how some of this work gets done, but most of that intelligence stays stuck inside the customer experience function. A health score might flag an at-risk account, but unless a customer success manager picks up the phone and personally tells the sales team, nobody adjusts the expansion strategy.

Sentiment analysis might catch a wave of complaints about a specific feature, but the product team won't hear about it until the next quarterly review. A customer's usage might drop off a cliff and trigger an alert inside the success platform, but marketing keeps sending promotional emails like nothing happened.

The insights are there. The predictions are accurate. The problem is that none of it automatically triggers action anywhere else in the organization.

The tools might look different from what you saw in the sales section, but the underlying problem is exactly the same. Customer experience platforms stack up over time. AI features get layered on top. Individual teams get faster and more efficient at their own piece of the work. But the flow between teams stays broken unless someone deliberately decides to fix it.

What comes next follows the same pattern you have already seen: four layers that show how customer experience evolves from reactive support into a system where customer feedback does not just inform decisions across the organization (see Table 5.3). It drives them automatically.

You will know how close you are to a fully connected customer experience stack when you can answer these questions honestly.

Table 5.3 The customer experience stack layers

Layer	What this layer controls	Basic setup	AI features turned on	Actually connected
Customer Data & Identity	Customer profiles live in CRM (Salesforce, HubSpot), support tools (Zendesk, Intercom), and analytics platforms.	Teams check dashboards manually to see account health and history.	Tools like Gainsight predict churn risk. Analytics flag usage drops automatically.	Churn signals auto-adjust marketing campaigns and trigger sales outreach. Usage data syncs across all systems in real time.
Feedback & Customer Voice	Surveys collect NPS scores. Support tickets get reviewed periodically.	Feedback is sorted by hand and discussed in quarterly meetings.	Platforms like Qualtrics auto-tag themes and detect sentiment in tickets and calls. Volume becomes manageable.	Complaint patterns automatically update product priorities. Negative trends adjust email messaging. Promoters feed into referral campaigns.

Service, Support, & Customer Journey	Support handles tickets via email, chat, and phone. Customer success tracks renewals manually.	Handoffs between teams happen manually through emails and internal notes.	Chatbots (Intercom, Drift) deflect routine questions. Health scores predict renewal risk. AI categorizes tickets.	Support issues auto-notify product teams. Renewal risk adjusts ad targeting. Onboarding problems update how you message new prospects.
Experience Design & Personalization	Self-service portals have knowledge articles. Experiences use predefined customer segments.	Rules are set manually and updated slowly.	Tools like Dynamic Yield personalize experiences based on behavior. AI chat handles complex issues. Search finds answers automatically.	Personalization updates based on churn and expansion signals. Advocacy programs trigger from promoter scores. Experience data feeds marketing and product teams.

- Does a churn signal in your success platform automatically change how marketing talks to that account?
- When a customer complains about a specific feature three times in a month, does that information reach the product team without someone manually forwarding it?
- If a customer's usage drops, does your sales team find out before they pitch an expansion?
- When a support issue reveals a pattern that affects onboarding, does that pattern update how you message new prospects, or does it sit in a report until someone has time to read it?

If most of those answers are no, you are not behind. You are just still operating in the second or third column.

When you build toward that fourth column, customer experience stops being the team that reacts to what everyone else did wrong. It becomes the system that automatically pushes what it learns back into sales, marketing, and product before the next customer ever has the same problem.

None of this requires you to rip everything out and start over. But it does require you to stop treating your stack like something that happened to you and start treating it like something you are choosing every single day.

If a tool earns its place in that fourth column, keep it. If it only exists because removing it feels like too much work, that is your answer. The goal is to have the right tools doing the right things across every team, without someone in the middle manually holding it all together.

Three Decisions That Close the Gap

Now that you understand what a good marriage with your tech stack looks like, the question becomes who is responsible for making that marriage work. The tools are ready and the AI features are there, but none of that matters if nobody has made the structural decisions that allow everything to connect.

Who owns the definitions your teams are working from, who owns the triggers that move information between departments, and who is accountable when the whole thing falls apart are the three decisions that determine whether you stay stuck in column 3 or actually make it to column 4.

Shared Definitions

Every team in your organization needs to be working from the same language, and that language needs to live inside your systems rather than in a slide deck someone presented 6 months ago. A qualified lead cannot mean one thing in marketing and something completely different in sales. A churn signal cannot exist only inside a customer success dashboard where no one else ever sees it.

These definitions need to be centralized, built into the logic of your tools, and applied the same way everywhere they show up. If you skip this step and start automating workflows before your teams even agree on what the stages mean, you are not scaling efficiency—you are scaling disagreement.

How to Start

Pick the one life cycle stage that causes the most confusion or finger-pointing between teams right now. For most organizations, that is either the definition of a qualified lead or what counts as an at-risk account. Get the two or three teams who touch that stage into a room and agree on a single definition, including what specific criteria have to be met before something moves into that stage and what happens next when it does. Once you have that, build it directly into your CRM system or success platform as a required field, a drop-down, or a stage gate so that it cannot be skipped or interpreted differently by different people. In tools like Salesforce or HubSpot, this means configuring pipeline stages with required fields that enforce the definition before a record can move forward.

If you are an individual contributor and you do not have the authority to change system settings, you can still document the misalignment, show where it is creating problems, and bring that to whoever manages the tool. Most of the time, the reason definitions stay broken is not because people disagree. It is because nobody has put the actual discrepancy in front of the right person with a clear recommendation for how to fix it.

System Triggers

When something meaningful happens in one system, it should automatically trigger the right response in another system without anyone needing to relay that information manually. If a lead score drops below a certain threshold, routing should change on its own without a meeting about it.

If churn risk increases on an account, product and marketing should be notified immediately instead of finding out at the next quarterly review. If adoption of a specific feature suddenly spikes or drops off, messaging should adjust based on that signal without waiting for someone to notice it in a report.

This requires workflow automation that crosses departmental tools instead of stopping at departmental boundaries, and without it, AI will keep making individual tasks faster without ever improving how your teams coordinate with each other.

How to Start

Map out the three to five moments in your customer life cycle where one team's action or insight should immediately inform what another team does next. Write them down as simple if-then statements.

If churn risk goes above a certain score, then pause promotional emails and notify the account owner.

If a support ticket volume spikes on a specific feature, then flag it for the product team. If a new customer has not completed onboarding within the first two weeks, then trigger a personalized outreach sequence. Once you have those statements written out, look at whether your current tools can automate them natively or whether you need a connector like Zapier, Make, or a built-in integration to bridge the gap between platforms.

Start with one trigger that crosses one departmental boundary and get it running reliably before you try to build 10 at once. If you are earlier in your career and do not control the automation layer, document the handoff that is currently breaking down, estimate what it is costing in time or lost accounts, and present that to the person who does control the tools. A clearly defined problem with a specific proposed trigger is much harder to ignore than a general complaint about communication between teams.

Data Ownership

Someone has to own how your systems connect, and it needs to be the person or team responsible for the outcomes those systems are supposed to produce. In a lot of organizations, IT ends up owning the tools by default because they are the ones who set them up, manage the licenses, and handle the technical side of keeping everything running. But IT does not own the sales process and they do not own the customer journey. They are not the ones held accountable when churn goes up or when leads fall through the cracks.

So, when the people who own the tools are completely disconnected from the people who own the outcomes, nobody is truly responsible for whether the system actually works the way it should from end to end. Ownership needs to sit with whoever is accountable for how customers move through the business, not whoever happened to configure the platform. That does not mean eliminating specialization across teams; it means aligning that specialization so that every department is building toward the same life cycle instead of building separate ones.

How to Start

Look at who currently has admin access to your core platforms and ask whether those people are also responsible for the business outcomes those platforms are supposed to drive. If the answer is no, that is your first gap. The fix is not to take access away from IT or operations, because you still need them for the technical management. The fix is to establish a life cycle owner, whether that is a revenue operations leader, a chief customer officer, or even a cross-functional working group who has the authority to make decisions about how systems connect and how data flows between departments.

If that role does not exist in your organization yet, you can start smaller by identifying one process that spans multiple teams, like the handoff from sales to onboarding, and assigning a single person to own how that handoff works across every tool it touches.

If you are an individual contributor, the most powerful thing you can do is document where the lack of ownership is creating real problems, things like conflicting data between systems, duplicated work, or decisions being made off outdated information, and bring that documentation to leadership with a clear proposal for who should own the connection point. Organizations rarely fix ownership problems until someone makes the cost of not fixing them visible.

When all three of these decisions are in place, the gap between those separate pyramids starts to collapse. AI stops functioning as a tool that makes individual departments faster and starts functioning as the connective tissue between them. Productivity shifts from how much each team can output on its own to how smoothly the entire life cycle operates from end to end.

That is the core argument of this book put into practice. AI treated as infrastructure instead of a collection of point tools, definitions aligned across every team, repetition automated so people stop doing it manually, and judgment protected so the work that requires human thinking stays with humans. That is how AI becomes durable leverage for your organization instead of just a faster way to create noise.

Chapter 6

AI ROI

You just spent time understanding how your tech stack connects, who owns it, and what it looks like when marketing, sales, and customer experience are working together instead of operating in silos. Now here is the question that most people cannot answer yet: If your boss came to you today and asked you to prove what your AI tools have accomplished, could you give them metrics that go beyond how much time you saved or how many tasks you automated?

Could you show them how AI changed the number of qualified leads entering the pipeline, or how it reduced churn in the first 90 days of a customer relationship, or how it shortened the gap between a support issue being identified and the product team actually fixing it?

Most people cannot, and that is not because AI is not doing anything. It is because nobody set up a way to measure whether the work AI is doing connects to the outcomes the business cares about. The activity is there. The adoption is there. What is missing is the bridge between what AI is doing inside each team and what the organization is trying to accomplish across all of them.

Most companies are tracking how much AI is being used when they should be tracking what that usage is changing. There is a real difference between measuring activity and measuring impact, and until you understand that difference, every dollar your organization spends on AI tools is an investment nobody can defend.

The first thing most teams measure when they adopt AI is how much time it saves, and on the surface that makes sense. If a task that used to take 30 minutes now takes 3, that feels like proof that the tool is working. The problem is that time saved on its own does not tell you anything about whether the business is better off.

If you automated a follow-up email that used to take 10 minutes to write but that email still gets ignored because it is going to the wrong person at the wrong stage of the buying process, you did not create value. You just created the wrong output faster. If you cut the time it takes to update your CRM system by 80 percent but the data going into the CRM system is still inconsistent across teams, you saved time entering information that nobody trusts enough to act on anyway.

Time saved is the most visible sign that AI is doing something, which is exactly why it becomes a trap. Teams report it because it is easy to count, leadership accepts it because it sounds impressive, and nobody asks the harder question, which is whether the time that was saved changed an outcome that matters.

A sales team that processes leads in 3 minutes instead of 30 is not necessarily closing more deals. A marketing team that produces five times more content is not necessarily generating better pipeline. A support team that responds to tickets twice as fast is not necessarily reducing churn. Speed is only valuable when it is attached to a result, and most organizations stop measuring before they get to the result.

This does not mean time saved is meaningless; it is just a starting point, not a finish line. The real question is what happened because of the time you got back, and if you cannot answer that, your ROI story has a hole in it that will eventually catch up with you.

If time saved is the starting point, outcomes are the destination. And the outcomes that matter most are the ones that cross departmental boundaries, because those are the ones that prove your systems are connected rather than just individually faster.

Here is a framework for thinking about what to measure at each stage of the life cycle. Instead of asking "How much time did AI save my team?," ask "What changed in the business because AI was involved?"

The metric most marketing teams default to is volume. How many leads did we generate, how many emails did we send, how many impressions did we get? With AI those numbers almost always go up, which makes it look like things are working. But the outcome that matters is whether the leads entering the pipeline are better qualified, whether they convert at a higher rate, and whether the campaigns that generated them were informed by data from sales and customer experience.

Think about this in three stages. When you are crawling, you are tracking the basics quantitatively: things like how many leads came in this month, what your cost per lead is, and how many emails or ads you produced. On the qualitative side, you are asking your sales team whether the leads marketing is sending over feel like they are getting better or worse, and you are paying attention to whether reps are following up on what marketing generates or quietly ignoring it.

Most teams live here for a long time and never move past it because these numbers are easy to pull and they look good on a slide.

When you start walking, you shift to conversion focused metrics. On the quantitative side, you are tracking the conversion rate from marketing qualified lead to sales accepted lead, how long it takes for a lead to move from first touch to pipeline, and what percentage of marketing sourced leads eventually turn into revenue. On the qualitative side, you are looking at whether marketing and sales agree on what a qualified lead looks like, and whether the campaigns generating the most volume are also generating the most pipeline or if those are two completely different lists.

When you are running, marketing ROI is tied directly to life cycle outcomes. Quantitatively you are measuring revenue influenced by marketing across the full customer journey, not just first touch attribution.

You are tracking how marketing campaigns perform differently when they are informed by churn data from customer experience or win and loss data from sales. Qualitatively you are evaluating whether marketing is operating as a stand-alone function that throws leads over the wall or whether it is a connected part of a system where campaign strategy is continuously shaped by what sales and customer experience are learning in real time.

Experiment: AI Lead Scoring and Routing

Now let's put this into practice with an actual test you can run (see Table 6.1). Say your marketing team is generating a healthy volume of leads but sales keeps complaining that half of them are unqualified, and the ones that are qualified sit untouched for 2 days because nobody knows which ones to call first.

Table 6.1 Scoring and routing

Component	Details
Objective	Increase the percentage of marketing qualified leads that sales accepts by using AI scoring to prioritize and route leads automatically instead of letting reps sort through them manually.
Hypothesis	If we implement AI lead scoring that evaluates fit and intent signals and automatically routes high scoring leads to the right rep within one hour of capture, the MQL-to-SQL conversion rate will increase from 18% to 32%.

Component	Details
Primary Metric	MQL-to-SQL conversion rate. Baseline: 18%. Target: 32%.
Supporting Metrics	Average time from lead capture to first sales contact. Number of leads untouched for more than 48 hours. Cost per qualified opportunity.
Volume	600 inbound leads per month. 180 qualified leads per month. $25,000 average deal size.
Time to Test	One full quarter.
ROI Calculation	If conversion rate increases from 18 to 32%, that is roughly 25 additional qualified opportunities per month. At a 20% close rate and $25,000 average deal size, that is $125,000 in additional pipeline per month or $375,000 over the test quarter.

Even if the numbers come in lower than projected, the experiment gives you a real baseline to iterate from instead of guessing.

Did AI Change How Efficiently Deals Move Through the Pipeline?

Sales teams tend to measure activity. Calls made, emails sent, meetings booked. AI makes all of those numbers go up. But the outcome that matters is whether deals are moving through the pipeline faster, whether win rates are improving, and whether the intelligence AI is surfacing about accounts is changing how reps prioritize their time.

At the crawl stage, you are measuring the quantitative basics like number of calls made, emails sent, meetings booked, and proposals delivered. These are activity metrics and AI will almost certainly make all of them go up, which is why they feel like progress. On the qualitative side you are asking reps whether AI tools are helping them have better conversations or just helping them have more conversations, and whether the information AI is surfacing about accounts feels accurate and useful or like noise they have to sort through.

At the walk stage, you move into pipeline efficiency. Quantitatively you are tracking average sales cycle length, win rate on qualified opportunities, and the ratio of proposals sent to deals closed. You are measuring whether deals are moving faster or whether reps are just busier.

Qualitatively you are evaluating whether AI-generated insights are changing how reps prioritize their pipeline, whether managers are coaching differently based on AI-surfaced patterns, and whether the team can articulate specifically what AI changed about how they sell rather than just saying it saves them time.

At the run stage, sales metrics connect directly to the full life cycle. Quantitatively you are tracking revenue per rep, customer lifetime value of deals closed with AI-assisted selling versus without, and how often AI identified expansion opportunities convert.

Qualitatively you are looking at whether intelligence from customer experience is flowing back into how sales approaches renewals and upsells, whether churn patterns are informing which deals sales pursues in the first place, and whether the sales process has fundamentally changed shape because of what AI is making visible rather than just getting faster at the same shape it always had.

Experiment: AI-Assisted Deal Prioritization and Follow-up

Here is a test you can run on the sales side (see Table 6.2). Say your reps are managing 50 or more active opportunities at any given time, and the biggest problem is not that they are not working hard enough but that they are spending equal time on every deal instead of focusing on the ones most likely to close. Deals stall out because nobody catches the early warning signs, and follow-ups happen on a schedule instead of in response to what the buyer is actually doing.

You are not trying to hit the target perfectly on the first attempt. What matters is that you now have a real number to measure against, because without that baseline you have no way of knowing whether AI is changing outcomes or just making your team look busier.

Table 6.2 Deal prioritization

Component	Details
Objective	Increase win rate on qualified opportunities by using AI to surface deal risk signals and prioritize rep activity based on buyer engagement patterns instead of gut feeling.
Hypothesis	If we use AI to flag deals where engagement has dropped or where a buying signal has appeared and automatically prompts reps with a recommended next action within 24 hours, win rate on qualified opportunities will increase from 22% to 31%.
Primary Metric	Win rate on qualified opportunities. Baseline: 22%. Target: 31%.

(continued)

Table 6.2 Continued

Component	Details
Supporting Metrics	Average sales cycle length in days. Percentage of stalled deals that reengage after AI prompted outreach. Number of deals where AI surfaced a signal the rep had not identified on their own.
Volume	200 active qualified opportunities per quarter. $40,000 average deal size. $1,760,000 current quarterly revenue from closed deals.
Time to Test	One full sales cycle, typically 60 to 90 days.
ROI Calculation	If win rate increases from 22% to 31%, that is roughly 18 additional closed deals per quarter at $40,000 each, representing $720,000 in additional revenue. Even a partial improvement to 26% translates to 8 additional deals and $320,000 in new revenue.

Customer experience teams often measure response time and ticket resolution speed, and AI almost always improves both. But the outcome that matters is whether customers are staying longer, expanding their usage, and becoming advocates.

At the crawl stage, you are tracking the quantitative basics like average response time, ticket resolution time, and customer satisfaction scores on individual interactions. These numbers will improve quickly once AI is involved, which makes it tempting to stop here.

Qualitatively you are asking whether customers feel like the support experience has gotten better or just faster, whether the answers AI is generating are accurate and helpful or generic and frustrating, and whether your team is spending more of their time on complex human problems now that routine tickets are being handled automatically.

At the walk stage, you shift toward retention and health metrics. Quantitatively you are tracking churn rate within the first 90 days, net revenue retention, the percentage of at risk accounts that received a proactive intervention before the customer raised the issue themselves, and how often AI-generated health scores accurately predicted which accounts were in trouble.

Qualitatively you are evaluating whether your team is using AI insights to have fundamentally different conversations with customers or just having the same conversations sooner, and whether the customer success team can point to specific accounts that were saved because of something AI surfaced that would have otherwise gone unnoticed.

At the run stage, customer experience metrics feed directly into the rest of the organization. Quantitatively you are tracking how support and usage data influence product development timelines, how churn signals adjust marketing messaging and sales outreach in real time, and what percentage of your expansion revenue comes from accounts where AI identified the opportunity before the customer asked for it.

Qualitatively you are assessing whether customer experience has shifted from being a reactive function that absorbs problems to a proactive system that prevents them, and whether the insights generated by customer interactions are changing decisions in other departments or just being reported and ignored.

Experiment: AI-Driven Upsell Triggers from Product Usage

Here is a test for the customer experience side (see Table 6.3). Say your team knows that when a customer hits a certain usage threshold or starts adopting a feature set that aligns with a higher-tier plan, there

Table 6.3 Tracking upsell from product usage

Component	Details
Objective	Increase upsell conversion rate by acting on product usage signals in real time instead of waiting for quarterly reviews.
Hypothesis	If we trigger automated expansion alerts based on usage spikes and route them to account owners within 24 hours, upsell conversion will increase from 7% to 14%.
Primary Metric	Upsell conversion rate. Baseline: 7%. Target: 14%.
Supporting Metrics	Time from usage spike to outreach. Number of expansion conversations initiated per quarter. Revenue per account after upsell.
Volume	500 existing customers. 200 expansion opportunities per quarter. $10,000 average expansion deal size.
Time to Test	One full quarter.
ROI Calculation	At 7% baseline on 200 opportunities, you close 14 upsells for $140,000 in expansion revenue. At 14%, that doubles to 28 upsells and $280,000, an additional $140,000 per quarter from customers you already have.

is usually an expansion opportunity. But right now that information lives in a product analytics dashboard that nobody on the success team checks regularly, and by the time someone notices the pattern, the customer has either figured it out on their own or the moment has passed.

The cost of setting up the usage trigger and routing automation is almost certainly a fraction of that return, which makes this one of the easiest experiments to justify because you are not acquiring new customers. You are just capturing revenue that was already sitting inside your existing base waiting for someone to act on it.

This is the metric most organizations never think to track, but it is the one that proves your systems are actually connected. It is also the one that ties directly back to everything you built in the previous chapters about shared definitions, system triggers, and data ownership.

At the crawl stage you are simply measuring whether information is crossing departmental boundaries at all. Quantitatively, track how many times per week a signal from one department results in any kind of action in another department, even if that action is manual.

How many times did customer experience flag something that sales actually heard about? How many times did a marketing insight reach the product team? Qualitatively, ask each team whether they feel like they know what the other departments are learning or whether they are operating with a completely separate view of the customer.

At the walk stage you start measuring speed and reliability. Quantitatively, track the average time between a signal appearing in one system and an action being taken in another. How many hours pass between a churn signal firing and the sales team being notified? How many days pass between a support complaint pattern emerging and the product team adding it to their backlog?

Qualitatively, evaluate whether these handoffs are happening because of system triggers you built or because someone remembered to send an email, and whether the information arriving in the other department is specific enough to act on or so vague that it gets deprioritized.

At the run stage, cross-functional metrics become the primary way you measure AI ROI. Quantitatively you are tracking end to end lifecycle metrics like total time from first touch to full customer activation, revenue impact of cross-departmental interventions, and the percentage of customer life cycle transitions that happen automatically without manual coordination.

Qualitatively you are evaluating whether your organization genuinely operates as an integrated system where intelligence flows continuously between teams, or whether it still operates as a collection of departments that occasionally share information when someone has the time and motivation to do it. If that gap is not shrinking, your AI tools are making departments faster in isolation without improving how they work together.

Experiment: Cross-Departmental Signal Routing

This is the experiment that ties everything together (see Table 6.4). Say your customer experience team regularly identifies complaint patterns about a specific feature, but that information takes weeks to reach the product team. Meanwhile marketing is still promoting that feature in campaigns, sales is still pitching it as a differentiator, and new customers are onboarding into an experience that existing customers are already frustrated with.

The actual number will depend on how quickly teams act once they receive the signal, which is why the qualitative side of this experiment matters just as much as the quantitative side. If the signal arrives faster but nobody changes their behavior in response, the automation is not the problem—the culture is. This experiment exposes both.

From Proof Points to a Portfolio

Once you have run a few of these tests and have real numbers attached to real outcomes, the next step is organizing them into something that tells a coherent story. Most organizations that struggle

Table 6.4 Cross-department signal routing

Component	What you define
Objective	Reduce the time between a customer complaint pattern emerging in support and that signal reaching product, marketing, and sales teams so they can adjust their actions accordingly.
Hypothesis	If we create automated triggers that route complaint pattern data from the support platform to product, marketing, and sales systems within 48 hours of a trend being detected, the average time from pattern emergence to cross-departmental awareness will decrease from 34 days to under 5 days.
Primary Metric	Average days from complaint pattern detection to cross-departmental action. Baseline: 34 days. Target: under 5 days.
Supporting Metrics	Number of marketing campaigns adjusted based on support data. Number of product backlog items created directly from automated support signals. Churn rate on accounts affected by the identified issue before and after the trigger is in place. Number of sales conversations where reps were aware of the issue before the prospect raised it.

(continued)

Table 6.4 Continued

Component	What you define
Volume	1,200 support tickets per month. 8 to 12 identifiable complaint patterns per quarter. $150,000 to $400,000 average revenue at risk per pattern if unaddressed.
Time to Test	One full quarter.
ROI Calculation	If even three complaint patterns per quarter reach the right teams 29 days earlier and each pattern puts an average of $250,000 in revenue at risk, the potential impact is $750,000 in protected revenue per quarter.

to justify their AI investment do not have a data problem—they have a narrative problem.

The proof points exist somewhere, scattered across different teams and different tools, but nobody has pulled them together into a single view that shows how AI is affecting the business as a whole.

Build a simple portfolio that tracks every AI initiative you have tested, what outcome it targeted, what the baseline was, what the result was, and what the financial impact turned out to be. It does not need to be complicated. A shared document or a dashboard with one row per initiative is enough.

The point is to have a single place where anyone in the organization can see what AI is actually doing rather than what people assume it is doing (see Table 6.5).

When you can show a table like this to leadership, the conversation about AI investment changes completely. You are no longer talking about how many hours people saved or how many more

Table 6.5 Proof Points

Initiative	Department	Outcome metric	Baseline	Result	Impact
AI lead scoring and routing	Marketing → Sales	Time from MQL to first sales contact	48 hours	3.5 hours	14% increase in conversion rate
Churn signal triggers proactive outreach	CX → Sales	At-risk accounts receiving intervention within 24 hours	22%	78%	15 accounts saved, $310K annual revenue retained
Support pattern detection feeds product backlog	CX → Product	Days between complaint pattern emerging and product team awareness	34 days	3 days	Top complaint resolved 2 months earlier than previous cycle

emails went out. You are talking about revenue retained, pipeline velocity, and cross-functional coordination that did not exist before.

That is how you defend every dollar in your tech stack, and that is how you make the case for the next investment when the time comes. A fillable version of this test template, ready to use for your first AI experiment, is available at `http://myaiworkweek.com/roitemplate`.

Decision Rules

That last experiment is a good example of something important. You can build the trigger, route the signal, and get the information to the right team in record time, but if the decision about what to do next is still unclear, the speed does not matter. Every experiment you run needs a decision rule built into it before you start, not after the results come in.

Something simple like if upsell conversion increases by at least 5 percentage points within one quarter, the automation gets scaled across all segments, and if it does not, you adjust the scoring thresholds and trigger timing and run the test again. Without that rule defined upfront, teams will spend weeks debating what the results mean instead of acting on them.

Once ROI is measurable, how you prioritize changes completely. You stop chasing features because a vendor showed you a compelling demo, you stop layering new tools on top of tools you have not fully used yet, and you stop reacting to whatever sounds exciting in the moment.

Instead you start making decisions based on what the data from your own experiments already told you is working, and that shift from reacting to deciding is what separates organizations that accumulate tools from organizations that actually get value out of them.

At this point you might be thinking that all of this sounds clean on paper, and you would be right. Templates always look organized in a document. Hypotheses always read well when they are sitting inside a nicely formatted table. But none of it means anything unless someone commits to running the experiment and following through on what the results tell them.

So let me tell you where $25 million in pipeline came from, because it did not come from a new ad campaign. It did not come from hiring more sales reps. It did not come from purchasing another platform or enabling another AI feature. It came from running one of these experiments with full commitment and letting the results reshape how the entire team operated.

Let me take you back to 2021. My schedule was the same every week. I had forecast calls, campaign reviews, and other regular meetings. But after the last big meeting, everything changed. Leaders said marketing and sales had to work together more closely. Their solution was a weekly meeting to review deals.

On paper, that sounds reasonable. The idea of closer alignment between sales and marketing had merit. In practice, however, it became a pressure cooker.

Every week, we had the same meeting with the same people. Even before the meeting started, people felt tense. Marketing brought charts and numbers. Sales shared stories from their work. The two-person data team rushed to make reports that both groups would trust. But no one trusted the reports. Everyone trusted what they saw themselves.

Fatigue was palpable. Reps were stressed. Managers were defensive. Some quietly disengaged, dreading the next hostile call even more than the last.

One particular week, I remember listening to the head of Sales for the Americas explain, again, that the leads marketing had qualified that month were "bad." Not misrouted. Not mistimed. Just bad. They did not match what Sales considered a real opportunity.

Before anyone could open the latest dashboard, the CMO was already pushing back. Volume targets had been hit. Cost per lead was down. Campaign performance looked strong. From marketing's perspective, they had delivered exactly what they were asked to deliver.

Now, I was brought in to evaluate how AI and automation could strengthen the revenue pipeline. Since it was my first time on the call, I came in with a student mindset. I needed to ask questions, even the basic ones. So I asked if we had ever compared the traits of deals that closed to the ones still in the pipeline after four months.

It wasn't some brilliant breakthrough. Looking back, it was an obvious question. But no one had put it that way before. The conversation usually circled around lead volume, attribution, or activity. Rarely did anyone stop to consider whether the system itself was rewarding the wrong things.

That question changed the direction of the next 90 days. Instead of debating lead quality in the abstract, we went into the CRM system. We pulled every closed-won deal from the last 4 months. All of them. Then we pulled every open deal that had been sitting for 6–8 months. And instead of manually arguing over spreadsheets, we used AI to summarize patterns across both groups.

Here's what stands out to me: In all those calls about pipeline and the never-ending debate of marketing versus sales leads, no one had ever bothered to pull up a simple Excel report of the accounts we actually won. I'm talking about a list with the exact numbers and names of contacts per account, side by side with our current pipeline.

It's a lot easier to see what matters when you have two Excel tabs open. For example, when we did this, we noticed that every deal we closed in the last 4 months had one thing in common—the CFO joined the sales negotiation calls when it was time to discuss pricing and contracts.

Just taking that one insight, we compared it to another sheet showing the current accounts that were stalling. Out of 17 accounts that had a contract discussion call, only 9 had the CFO present. So, we dug into the account notes to figure out why the CFOs were missing. The reasons were usually pretty normal: the CFO was busy, the company had just lost its CFO, or the CFO was still onboarding.

All understandable, but these day-to-day issues were actually huge blockers in our sales pipeline.

So, for the next alignment call, we made a plan. We took both Excel sheets, scrubbed out the account and contact details, and asked the AI to generate a checklist of what the current deals were missing—using only the last 4 months of won deals as the reference point.

In 10 minutes, we had a game plan: For accounts without a CFO, bring in someone who speaks a lot with finance, such as a CRO, a finance lead for sales, or a sales analyst. They're likely to join calls with sales and finance teams when tools are being considered. Bringing them in early makes it much easier to win them over during actual contract talks.

For the two accounts where the CFO was too busy, we launched a targeted campaign—blogs, whitepapers with podcast embeds they could listen to instead of reading, and an ROI calculator tailored to CFOs.

The calculator let them see, in just a few clicks, how much money they could save and how quickly they'd see results after onboarding. We sent those materials to the busy CFOs, tracked their engagement, and followed up to show how fast we could implement the software and deliver ROI.

Within 60 days of launching those materials, both stalled deals moved forward. And over the next 3 months, after going back to the other six accounts and adding the missing contacts, we closed three of the six. Sometimes, it's not about a new tool or a bigger pipeline. It's about seeing what's right in front of you and building your next move around it.

As silly as it sounds, you need people in every AI discussion who can actually make a decision at the end of it. If they're in leadership, own the process, or are directly responsible for the outcome, they need to be in the room. The truth is, once you start making progress with AI, you will uncover inefficiencies. And when you do, you can't wait for a perfect answer; someone needs to act.

Decision fatigue is real, so prep your leadership teams to act on solutions and not just wait for more data or hold out until the system is flawless. Progress comes from making the call, not just spotting the problem.

Chapter 7

Building a Sustainable System

Managers face a parallel challenge that most leadership training has never prepared for. When one employee becomes proficient with AI, the internal dynamics of a team shift in ways that are hard to name but impossible to ignore. Expectations rise unevenly, anxiety spreads quietly, and the social fabric of the team begins to stretch in new directions.

The AI-proficient employee often feels pressure to maintain their edge while others feel threatened or left behind. Leaders tend to underestimate this psychological layer because it does not show up in productivity dashboards or project timelines. It surfaces in hallway conversations, in the hesitation before someone asks a question, and in the low hum of tension that follows a team meeting where AI came up.

In this chapter, you'll learn how to spend time on what matters.

Dealing With AI Fatigue

AI fatigue is real, and it accumulates faster than most managers expect. Tool switching, prompt refinement, experimentation, and continuous learning all create cognitive overhead that does not appear on any workload report. The excitement of early wins masks the strain building underneath, and by the time a team member hits a wall, they are often already behind.

Managers must normalize phased adoption and protect their teams from the pressure to implement everything at once. Not every function needs the same tools, and not every employee needs to be at the same stage of fluency at the same time. A sustainable system is one where the pace of adoption matches the capacity of the people doing the adopting.

Cognitive overload appears when teams operate across multiple AI tools without shared standards to anchor them. Switching between different interfaces, prompt styles, and output formats drains attention in ways that feel subtle but compound over time. Managers who limit the number of primary AI tools per function and define consistent usage norms give their teams something more valuable than access. They give them clarity.

The pressure of being labeled the AI champion on a team is subtle but powerful in its consequences. The individual who figures it out first becomes the default trainer, fixer, and experimenter for everyone around them. Without guardrails, that role expands well beyond what one person can sustainably carry, and the team loses both their productivity and their goodwill.

Managers must redistribute AI knowledge deliberately and build structures that prevent it from concentrating in one place. Shared prompt libraries, documented workflows, and rotating ownership of AI-related responsibilities spread the load and spread the learning. When knowledge lives in systems instead of individuals, the whole team gets stronger without burning anyone out.

There is also a political dimension to AI adoption that managers rarely discuss openly. Moving faster than peers can create resentment, and AI adopters sometimes unintentionally expose inefficiencies in colleagues who are still finding their footing. Managers must frame

AI acceleration as team leverage rather than individual superiority, because teams that compete internally rarely outperform teams that advance together.

Psychological sustainability depends on how consistently leaders return to a narrative of collective benefit. When people understand that AI fluency lifts the team rather than sorts it into winners and losers, resistance softens and adoption accelerates naturally. The framing a manager chooses in the early stages of this shift will shape the culture long after the tools themselves have changed.

There is a deeper responsibility here that goes beyond team dynamics, and it belongs to every manager navigating this moment. If you manage people, you are now a steward of their career resilience whether you signed up for that role or not. The professionals on your team are watching how you move through this shift, and they are drawing conclusions about their own futures based on what they see you do.

If you hoard AI knowledge, they fall behind. If you push adoption without support, they burn out. If you ignore the shift entirely, you leave them exposed to a market that will not wait for anyone to catch up at their own pace. These are not dramatic outcomes. They are the predictable results of ordinary management decisions made during an extraordinary moment.

The managers who earn lasting loyalty in this era will be the ones who made AI fluency a team asset instead of a personal advantage. They will be the ones who created shared systems, protected people from burnout, redistributed knowledge generously, and kept the focus on what the team could build together. That is not a management technique. That is a leadership obligation, and it is one of the most important ones this generation of managers will ever have the chance to meet.

Creating a Culture of Measured Acceleration

Managers should establish adoption phases and communicate clearly what each one requires from the team. The exploration phase is where curiosity is the job—where employees test tools, surface observations, and build personal familiarity without the pressure of producing results. A customer service team in the exploration phase might spend two weeks testing how different AI tools summarize support tickets, with no expectation that any of it will change their current process.

The pilot phase is where promising applications get tested against real workflows in a controlled way, with intentional evaluation built in from the start. A marketing team in this phase might use an AI writing assistant on one campaign while running another campaign the traditional way, then compare the quality of output, the time invested, and the team's experience doing the work.

The standardization phase is where what worked gets documented, shared, and built into team norms so that individual experiments become collective assets. A sales team that successfully piloted AI-generated call prep summaries, for example, would use standardization to turn that into a shared prompt template available to every rep, not just the one who figured it out first.

Each phase carries different expectations, and managers must make those expectations explicit rather than letting people guess. Not every experiment becomes policy, and not every early success is ready to scale. When teams understand that exploration is allowed to stay exploratory, they take smarter risks and surface more honest feedback.

Regular reflection sessions reduce fatigue in ways that no tool or workflow can replicate on their own. Teams should have dedicated space to discuss what is working, what feels heavy, and what should be paused without those conversations being treated as complaints or resistance.

An HR team rolling out AI for job description drafting might discover after a few weeks that the review and editing process is taking longer than writing from scratch ever did, and a reflection session is where that signal surfaces before it becomes a morale problem. Sustainable systems are built with a release valve, and managers who normalize slowing down when necessary protect their teams from the kind of compounding exhaustion that quietly kills adoption.

Recognition must shift from output volume to decision quality if a culture of measured acceleration is going to hold. When employees believe that faster always equals better, they optimize for speed at the expense of judgment, and burnout accelerates right alongside their output.

A customer service rep who uses AI to handle 50 tickets a day but flags three edge cases that prevent a billing error from reaching a hundred customers is doing better work than one who closes 80 tickets without stopping to think. When employees understand that thoughtful application is valued more than raw throughput, they make better decisions, flag problems earlier, and stay in the work longer.

A sustainable system is not defined by how much AI you deploy across your team or how quickly you reach full adoption. It is defined by how well you control AI's impact on your time, your focus, and the psychological health of the people doing the work. The teams that build something durable are the ones that treated sustainability as a design requirement from the beginning, not as something to address after the damage was already done.

Clarity Over Tool Sprawl

Before you evaluate a single AI tool, you need to understand the problem you are trying to solve. That sounds obvious, but most teams skip it. They hear about a tool that speeds up content creation or automates approvals, and they book a demo before they have ever written down what the current process looks like, who is doing it, and where it breaks. The result is a tool that solves a problem the vendor defined rather than the one the team is living with every day.

Start by naming the pain in plain language. Not a strategic objective. Not a KPI. A sentence that any new hire could read and immediately recognize as true.

Think about the way you grocery shop versus the way your partner does. You write the list before you leave the house. You organize it by section of the store, produce first, then dairy, then frozen, so you are never backtracking across the store. You are in and out in 35 minutes.

Your partner goes without a list, remembers things as they walk past them, doubles back three times, and spends an hour doing the same task.

Neither of you is wrong. You are both buying groceries. But one of you has a process and one of you is improvising, and that difference shows up every single week in time, energy, and the occasional argument about forgetting the pasta.

The same dynamic plays out in every team, in every department, in every company that has more than one person completing the same workflow.

Once you have named the pain, the next step is to find out where the process is documented. Ask your team where the written process lives. If no one can find it in under two minutes, that is already useful information.

A process that exists only in someone's memory is a process that lives and dies with the person who holds it, and it is also a process that has probably already drifted from whatever was originally intended.

Then go find the newest person on your team who is completing this workflow. Find the person who just joined and is learning it for the first time, still asking questions, still figuring out the unwritten rules. Ask them to record a short video walking through exactly how they complete the process today. Show where the request starts. Show where it goes. Show what gets filled out, who it gets sent to, and what happens next. Do not coach them. Do not correct them. Just ask them to show you what they actually do.

After that, go to the most senior person completing the same workflow. Someone who has been doing it long enough that it feels automatic. Ask them to record the same video under the same instructions. What you will find between those two recordings is the most honest picture of your process that any documentation has ever given you.

The written process, the new employee version, and the senior version will not match. They never do. Your job at this stage is only to notice that difference, not to judge it, not to let anyone on the call comment on how someone else is doing it, and not to treat either version as wrong. The gap between them is the data.

Now you have something real to work with. You have a named problem, a documented current state, and a clear picture of how the work actually moves through your organization today. Take the senior employee's recording, because it represents the most optimized human version of the process, and use it as your evaluation benchmark.

Sign an NDA with any vendor you are seriously considering. Then send them the video. Do not send a list of requirements. Do not send a feature wish list. Send them the video and ask them to respond with a written standard operating procedure showing what this same workflow would look like using their tool, with minimal disruption to how the work is currently structured. If they cannot do that, they are not solving your problem. They are selling you a new one.

A sales operations team can run the same process against a completely different pain point and arrive at the same clarity. Consider a revenue team where account executives are manually pulling together pre-call research from three different systems, a CRM, a LinkedIn profile, and a news search, before every discovery call. The process takes 20 minutes per rep per call, it is inconsistent across the team, and senior reps have developed shortcuts that newer reps do not know exist.

The pain statement is simple: Our reps spend too much time preparing for calls and the quality of that prep varies too much from person to person. Record the newest rep doing it. Record the most senior rep doing it. Notice where they diverge.

Then take the senior version to a vendor and ask them to show you, specifically, how their tool would compress that 20-minute process without requiring reps to move their work into a new system. If the answer requires a new dashboard, a new data entry step, or a weekly export to function, the tool is adding steps, not removing them.

This is what clarity over tool sprawl actually means in practice. It is not a philosophy—it is a sequence. Name the problem in plain language, find where the process is documented, record how two different people at different experience levels actually complete it, notice the gap without judging it, and then use the most optimized human version as the standard any AI tool must meet or beat.

The teams that follow this sequence before they ever open a browser tab to compare pricing plans are the ones who end up with tools that stick. Everyone else ends up with a subscription they are too busy to cancel and a workflow that is somehow more complicated than the one they started with.

By this point, you have probably tested more AI tools than you planned to. Some impressed you immediately. Others felt promising but complicated. A few required onboarding calls, documentation reading, and configuration work before they even produced value. That is where chaos begins.

Most professionals evaluate tools backward. They watch polished demos, imagine ideal use cases, and then try to bend their workflow around the tool. Sustainable operators do the opposite. They start with a finished workflow and challenge the tool to improve it without altering its structure.

Before you commit to any AI tool, give it 30 minutes to onboard, 30 minutes to connect to a relevant data source, and 30 minutes to produce an output for a real workflow you already run. If it cannot generate a usable output within that window, it does not qualify for deeper evaluation.

This rule does two important things: It protects your time from extended onboarding cycles, and it forces tools to prove immediate leverage rather than theoretical capability. You are not testing the tool's maximum potential—you are testing time to value.

Start with Your Workflow, Not Their Features

Before you contact any vendor, record yourself completing the workflow you want to improve. Keep it under five minutes. Show where the task starts, where data enters, where decisions get made, and where it slows down or breaks. This recording is your benchmark, and it is the only thing a vendor needs to understand your problem.

Do not book a demo. Demos are designed for the vendor, not for you. They show you the best version of the tool in the most favorable conditions against problems you may not even have. If a company has built a tool specifically meant to solve your problem, they already have videos showing it in action. Search for those first. Watch how the tool behaves in real workflows, not in staged presentations with clean data and a polished presenter controlling every click.

If you cannot find existing videos that match your use case closely enough, send the vendor your recording and ask them to respond with a short video showing exactly how their tool would handle your specific workflow. Any legitimate vendor can produce that in under five minutes.

If they push back and insist on a live discovery call instead, that tells you something. It means their tool requires explanation to look good, and tools that require explanation to look good usually require a lot more explanation once you are actually using them.

Ask Direct, Operational Questions

When you do reach out to a vendor, skip the open-ended questions and ask for specifics that reveal how the tool behaves when things do not go perfectly. Ask what happens when the tool produces a wrong output and how your team would know. Ask whether the tool requires someone to review every output before it is used or whether it is designed to act without a human checkpoint.

Ask how long it takes a new team member to use it independently without help from someone who already knows it. Ask what your team would do tomorrow if the tool went down, and whether the work could still get done.

These questions matter because they expose the real cost of adoption before you have committed to anything. A tool that requires daily human review of its outputs has not removed a step from your workflow—it has added one. A tool that works well only after weeks of internal training is a training program disguised as software.

If any answer includes the phrase "you would just need to" followed by a process change, slow down. That phrase is where hidden complexity lives, and every step a vendor describes as simple is a step your team will have to learn, maintain, and troubleshoot long after the vendor has moved on to their next sale.

Measure Time to Solution

The only metric that matters in early evaluation is time to solution, meaning how long it takes from the moment you start using the tool to the moment it produces something your team can actually use. Most people try to measure this by feel, and feel is not reliable. You will naturally be more patient with a tool you paid for, more forgiving of friction when you are excited about potential, and less likely to count the steps that happen in the background while you wait. You need a way to measure this that has no bias built into it.

Before you begin trialing any tool, open Glitter AI in the background. Glitter AI is a browser extension that runs quietly while you work and captures every click, every action, and every second of elapsed time as you move through a new workflow.

You are not narrating anything or setting up a recording session. You simply start using the tool and Glitter AI documents what actually happens. By the time you finish your first real use of the tool, you have an unedited record of how many steps it took, how long each one lasted, and where you slowed down or got stuck.

What you end up with is two things at once. You have your time to solution measured without anyone's opinion attached to it, including your own. And you have a draft standard operating procedure already built, because Glitter AI turns that recorded session into a documented workflow automatically.

If the tool takes longer to produce a usable output than your manual process did, you can see exactly where the time went and make a clear decision. If it is genuinely faster, you now have documentation ready to share with your team from day one of adoption.

Many tools compress one visible step while quietly expanding three others that nobody counted during the evaluation. Glitter AI counts them for you. The goal is not a tool that could save time under ideal conditions. The goal is a tool that saves time under your conditions, with your data, inside your team's actual day, and now you have the receipts to know whether it does.

Avoid Workflow Drift

Workflow drift happens slowly, and that is what makes it dangerous. You adopt a tool, it works well enough to keep, and then small adjustments start accumulating. You save files in a new place because the tool prefers it. You add a step to your process because the tool requires it. You open a new tab every morning to check what the tool is doing. None of these feel like big changes in the moment, but six months later your workflow looks completely different and nobody remembers deciding to change it.

The simplest test is this: Since adopting the tool, has your team added any steps, any locations, or any new places to check that did not exist before? If yes, the tool is not saving you work. It is creating it. A good AI tool should make your current process shorter, not give you a second process to manage alongside the first one.

Use the Replace Rule

The Replace Rule is built around one idea: Every tool you add should kill something else. Most teams treat new tools as additions. They bring in an AI writing assistant and still keep the old content brief template. They adopt an AI meeting summarizer and still take manual notes just in case. They add an AI prospecting tool and still run the old enrichment process in parallel because nobody officially turned it off. Before long the team is maintaining two versions of the same workflow and the new tool has not saved anyone any time. It has just added a layer on top of what already existed.

The Replace Rule forces a different decision. Before a tool goes live, you name specifically what it is replacing and you set a date for when that thing stops. Not eventually. Not once everyone is comfortable. On a specific date. If the AI tool is handling meeting summaries starting Monday, manual note-taking in that meeting ends Monday. If the AI tool is generating first drafts of outreach emails starting next week, the old copy-paste template library gets retired next week.

The reason this matters beyond just staying organized is that parallel systems hide the truth about whether a tool is actually working. If your team can always fall back on the old process, they will, especially when the new tool produces something imperfect. You never get real adoption data and you never get real time savings because the old process is quietly absorbing all the cases where the new tool falls short.

The secondary benefit is that the Replace Rule functions as a gut check during evaluation. If you cannot identify what the tool replaces clearly enough to commit to removing it, the tool is probably not solving a defined problem. It is filling a gap you have not fully named yet, and that is usually a sign to pause before purchasing.

Run a Live Use Case, Not a Hypothetical

Test every tool against real work from your team, not examples the vendor prepared for you. Vendor demo data is chosen because it makes the tool look good. Your data is messier, more specific, and shaped by decisions your team made long before this tool existed. That is exactly what makes it the only honest test.

Take an AI meeting summarizer as an example. The vendor demo will show you a clean 30-minute call with two speakers, clear audio, full sentences, and a tidy set of action items at the end. Your actual calls probably look nothing like that. Someone joined five minutes late and caught up out loud. Three people talked over each other during the most important part of the conversation.

Half the context lives in a shared document that nobody screen-shared. Someone referenced a decision from two weeks ago without explaining what it was. That is a normal call, and that is the call you need to run through the tool before you decide whether it belongs in your workflow.

If the summary it produces from that call is accurate and useful, you have real evidence. If it misses the key decision, attributes an action item to the wrong person, or produces something so generic it could apply to any meeting, that is a fit problem, not an onboarding problem. Fit problems do not get better with more training or more time. A tool that only performs well on a vendor's curated example is not ready for your team.

Keep the Evaluation Window Tight

Give every tool a fixed evaluation window of two weeks and track four specific things during that time. The first is how many usable outputs the tool actually produced, meaning outputs your team used, acted on, or sent without significant rework. A summary nobody read does not count.

A draft that required 30 minutes of editing before it was usable does not count. You are tracking finished value, not activity. The second is time saved compared to your manual baseline on the same tasks. If you do not have a manual baseline already recorded, go back to your Glitter AI session from the workflow mapping step and use that as your benchmark.

The third is how many times the integration with your existing systems failed, stalled, or required someone to intervene to get it working again. One failure in two weeks is a data point. Five failures in two weeks is a pattern. The fourth is how the team describes the cognitive load of using the tool.

Ask them directly. Does this feel lighter than what you were doing before, about the same, or heavier? That answer matters as much as any time metric because a tool that saves 10 minutes but creates 30 minutes of low-grade frustration is not a net positive.

To make this concrete, imagine your team is evaluating an AI tool that drafts follow-up emails after sales calls. In week 1, three reps use it on real calls. You track how many of those drafts went out with minimal edits, how long it took each rep to go from call end to sent email compared to their previous average, whether the CRM integration logged the emails correctly every time, and whether the reps describe the experience as easier or just different.

In week 2 you expand to five reps and look for consistency. Are the results holding or were the week 1 results beginner's luck from the reps who are most comfortable with new tools? At the end of two weeks you have real data from real use and a decision becomes straightforward.

If the leverage is clear, move toward standardization. If it is unclear after two full weeks of real use, remove the tool. Indefinite trials do not produce better data. They produce attachment, sunk cost reasoning, and a subscription that quietly renews for 18 months while everyone waits for the tool to finally click.

Intentional Tooling as Strategic Behavior

Before you go looking for a new AI tool, check what the tools you already use have built. Most of the platforms already living in your tech stack have released AI features in the last 12–18 months, and those features are worth evaluating first. The user experience is already familiar to your team. The data connections are already established. The login already exists. Adopting an AI feature inside a tool your team uses every day carries a fraction of the change management burden that adopting a net new platform does.

If you use HubSpot, check what their AI features can do before evaluating a separate AI prospecting tool. If your team lives in Notion, look at their AI capabilities before buying a stand-alone meeting summarizer. If you are already on Google Workspace or Microsoft 365, both have AI layers built in that most teams have not fully explored. The tool that fits most cleanly into your workflow is often the one already connected to the systems you rely on, not the one with the best landing page.

When you do need to evaluate something outside your existing stack, use G2.com to research the company behind the tool before you spend any time on the product itself. G2 lets you see who built it, how long they have been in market, how their other products are reviewed, and whether the company has a pattern of building tools that teams actually stick with.

A tool built by a company whose other products you already trust is a lower risk adoption than a tool built by a team you have never heard of with six months of reviews. The AI tool market is loud, and it is designed to make you feel behind. Your job is not to keep up with all of it. Your job is to solve a specific problem with the least amount of disruption possible, and that search almost always starts closer to home than you think.

Replacing Effort as Currency

For years, effort was the most visible sign of professional value. Long hours. Late night emails. A calendar packed from end to end. The ability to absorb more work than anyone around you and still respond within minutes. These were not just habits. They were proof—proof that you were committed, capable, and worth keeping.

Consider a project manager named Dana. For eight years, Dana's reputation was built on output. She could turn a project brief into a full status report, a risk matrix, and a stakeholder update in a single afternoon. Her manager trusted her because she was always first in and last out. Her peers respected her because nothing slipped. Dana's effort was visible every day, and that visibility was the foundation of her standing on the team.

Then the tools changed. The status report that took Dana three hours now takes 30 minutes with AI assistance. The risk matrix she used to build manually now generates in a single prompt. The stakeholder update she crafted carefully each week now drafts itself from her meeting notes. Dana is producing the same work in a fraction of the time, and she has no idea what to do with what is left.

This is the destabilization that most career development conversations are not prepared to address. When the proposal that once took eight hours now takes 90 minutes, visible strain disappears. The late nights are gone. The packed calendar starts to open up. And if effort was the currency Dana used to signal her value, she is now sitting in front of an empty register wondering what she has left to offer.

The answer is that she has more to offer than she ever did. She just has to learn to denominate it differently. Impact signals value now. Clarity signals value. Direction signals value. Dana still knows which risks actually matter on a project and which ones are noise. She still knows which stakeholder needs information framed a specific way to move forward.

She still knows when a project is technically on schedule but organizationally about to fall apart. AI did not learn any of that. Dana did, over eight years of doing the work. What changed is that the execution layer underneath those judgments got faster, which means Dana now has time to do the thing she was always too busy to do before. She can move upstream.

Moving upstream means shifting from the person who completes work to the person who shapes how work gets defined. For Dana, it looks like being in the room before the project brief exists rather than after. It looks like asking the questions that determine whether a project should be structured as three phases or six, whether the right stakeholder is in the loop before kickoff or after the first missed deadline, and whether the success metric the team agreed on in week 1 still reflects what the business actually needs in week 4.

None of that appears in a status report. All of it determines whether the project delivers anything worth reporting on.

Some professionals respond to this transition by doing the opposite of what Dana eventually did. They re-create visible effort to preserve perceived worth. They take on more tasks. They respond to messages instantly even when nothing is urgent. They inflate activity to fill the space that efficiency has created. Effort inflation feels safe because it looks like the thing that worked before, but it does not restore scarcity. It accelerates burnout and it signals to the people watching that you have not yet figured out where the real work lives now.

There is also a shift happening underneath the surface of career development itself. If AI compresses the time required to build competence in execution, traditional career timelines change with it. Research, drafting, modeling, competitive analysis—these are no longer gated by years of repetition alone.

A project manager two years into their career can now produce outputs that would have taken Dana five years to develop the speed and pattern recognition to create. That does not make Dana less valuable. It changes what her value is made of. Experience now compounds around judgment, consequence awareness, and the ability to see around corners, not around the mechanical repetition of tasks that a well-prompted model can now handle in seconds.

AI does not eliminate the need for work. It redistributes where the most consequential work lives. The professionals who thrive in this shift will not be the ones who clung to execution as identity. They will be the ones who recognized the migration early, understood where value was moving, and repositioned themselves before the market made the decision for them. Dana is one of them, and her transition is worth looking at directly before we move on.

What Dana Stopped Doing Because of AI

Status reports built from scratch are no longer on Dana's Sunday evening agenda. The risk matrices she used to assemble manually at the end of every planning sprint now generate in minutes. The stakeholder updates she once crafted word by word now draft themselves from her meeting notes and get reviewed rather than written. Stopping the execution did not mean abandoning the standard. It meant freeing the capacity to hold a higher one.

What Dana Owns Now

The conversations that happen before a project has a name are where Dana spends her time now. Leadership calls her when a new initiative is being scoped and nobody is sure yet whether it should be one project or three.

A monthly alignment session with department heads sits on her calendar, built specifically to surface the projects that are technically active but organizationally stalled, the ones where the status report says green and the hallway conversations say otherwise. Deciding which questions the team should be asking has become her job, not answering the questions after someone else already defined them.

What the Outcome Looks Like

Visibility did not decrease when Dana stepped back from execution. It changed shape. Conversations that used to happen two levels above her now include her. When leadership talks about who understands how work actually moves through the organization, her name comes up. The hours are no longer than they used to be. The rooms are just different, and the people in those rooms are starting to notice that the projects Dana touches tend to land differently than the ones she does not.

That is what upstream looks like in practice. It is not a title or a promotion. It is a shift in where your judgment gets applied and how early it arrives in the process. The question is not whether you can produce more. It is whether you can see where value now concentrates and move toward it deliberately, while you still have the runway to choose.

Spending Time on What Actually Matters

You do not need to take anyone's word for the fact that value is migrating upstream. You can see it happening right now in job descriptions. The language employers use when they write a job posting is one of the most honest signals available about what they are actually willing to pay for, and that language has been changing in ways that are hard to miss if you know what to look for.

A standard project manager job description from five years ago read like a list of execution tasks:

- Develop detailed project plans.
- Ensure resource availability and allocation.
- Deliver projects on time, within scope, and within budget.

- Track milestones.
- Prepare status reports.
- Submit progress updates to stakeholders.

The entire description was organized around the mechanics of completing work and producing documentation. The skills it asked for were organizational skills, time management, proficiency in Microsoft Project, and the ability to manage multiple tasks simultaneously. Nothing in that description was wrong. It accurately described what the job required at the time.

Current project manager postings from companies like Oracle, Deloitte, and OpenAI read differently. They ask for the ability to translate technical updates into strategic business impact for executive audiences. They ask for experience connecting project objectives to broader organizational goals. They ask for judgment in interpreting AI-generated insights rather than generating outputs manually. The role has shifted from manual tracking to interpreting AI-generated insights and making strategic decisions. The execution tasks are still there, but they are no longer the headline.

What sits at the top of the requirements now is judgment, cross-functional influence, and the ability to operate at the level where decisions get made rather than where deliverables get produced. It reflects a real change in what organizations need from the people they hire.

When AI handles the first draft of the status report, the project plan, and the risk matrix, the person in the role has capacity that did not exist before. The question companies are now asking in their hiring process is whether that person knows what to do with it. The three capabilities that keep surfacing in that answer are discernment, constraint setting, and integration.

Discernment

Most organizations are about to produce more content, more analysis, more dashboards, and more proposals than they ever have before. The surface area of work will expand in every direction. But volume does not equal clarity, and abundance creates noise faster than it creates progress. The individual who can look at 10 options and reduce them to two credible paths is not just being decisive. They are providing structural leverage that no AI tool can replicate on its own.

Discernment is not instinct. It is pattern recognition built from watching what kinds of decisions hold up under pressure and which ones look good in a document and fall apart in execution. AI can generate the options. It cannot carry the weight of knowing which ones have a history of working in your specific market, with your specific team, inside your specific constraints. That knowledge lives with you, and the more output AI produces, the more valuable your ability to filter it becomes.

Constraint Setting

If discernment determines which outputs matter, constraint setting determines what gets built in the first place. When AI is fed weak goals, it scales weak output. When it receives clear constraints, honest trade-offs, and a specific definition of success, the work it produces is actually usable. The person who defines those inputs shapes the system more than the person refining deliverables on the other end.

Constraint setting happens before a project starts, not after. It is the practice of asking what a successful outcome looks like in 30 days, what trade-offs the team is willing to accept, and what work will stop in order to make room for this one. Those questions feel simple and most teams skip them because they are eager to start producing. AI makes it even easier to start producing before the goal is clear, which means the cost of skipping constraint setting has gone up considerably.

The professional who slows a room down long enough to define the guardrails before the work begins is the person whose judgment the final output will reflect. Every hour spent clarifying what the team is optimizing for saves multiples of that hour downstream when the work would otherwise need to be redone because the goal shifted or was never clearly agreed upon in the first place.

Integration

Specialization built careers for decades because depth was hard to develop and therefore scarce. In an AI environment, depth of execution is more accessible than it has ever been. What remains genuinely difficult is the ability to move horizontally across functions and understand how the work in one area shapes the outcomes in another.

AI increases the surface area of visibility inside organizations. More data gets captured, more reports get generated, and more dashboards get built than any one person can meaningfully track. What AI does not do automatically is synthesize across those surfaces and identify what the connections mean.

The professional who understands how marketing data informs sales qualification, how product usage patterns predict churn, and how customer feedback shapes positioning is not just informed. They are connective tissue, and connective tissue is what holds an organization together when the volume of output gets high enough to create confusion instead of clarity.

Integration is not a role. It requires curiosity about what is happening outside your immediate lane, the habit of asking how your work affects the people downstream from you, and the willingness to bring a point of view into rooms where you are not the subject matter expert. In an AI-accelerated environment, those habits are the difference between a professional whose influence grows with the tools and one whose relevance narrows as the tools get better.

Discernment, constraint setting, and integration are not skills you develop by doing more of what you are already doing. They develop by deliberately shifting where your attention goes during the hours that AI has freed up. If the tool is handling the first draft, the question is what you do with the time you got back. If the analysis generates itself, the question is whether you use that time to evaluate it more carefully or simply to produce more of it.

The language in job postings is already showing you where the market is heading. The professionals who arrive there first are the ones who treated recovered time as an investment opportunity rather than a productivity bonus. They took the hours AI returned and put them into the conversation that needed to happen before the project started, the pattern hiding across three departments, or the decision everyone was avoiding because it required someone to take a position.

That is where the work is now. The question is whether you are spending your time there.

Attach Your Work to Revenue, Not Activity

Most professionals undersell their contributions not because the work lacks impact but because the language used to describe it stops at the task rather than the consequence. The difference between those two things is often the difference between being seen as someone who executes and being seen as someone who drives outcomes.

Leadership allocates resources to people who demonstrably influence revenue, reduce risk, or control cost. If you are not describing your work in those terms, you are making it harder for the right people to advocate for you even when they want to. Consider a CFO whose weekly update to the board reads something like this:

Version 1: Reviewed Q3 variance report. Completed month-end close. Attended vendor contract negotiation. Finalized headcount reconciliation for operations.

Every one of those items represents real work. None of them tell the board anything about why that work mattered or what would have happened without it. Read in sequence, they sound like a timesheet, and a timesheet does not build influence, justify resource decisions, or make the case for why this person belongs in strategic conversations.

Version 2: Identified a 14 percent variance in Q3 operating expenses tied to three vendor contracts that had auto-renewed at rates above market. Initiated renegotiations projected to recover $340,000 annually starting in Q4. Completed month-end close two days ahead of schedule, which allowed the leadership team to make a headcount decision before the end of the fiscal quarter rather than carrying the cost into next year. Flagged a reconciliation discrepancy in operations headcount that, left unaddressed, would have triggered a compliance review in the next audit cycle.

Same work. Same week. Completely different story. The first version describes activity. The second version describes consequence, and consequence is the only language leadership uses when it decides who belongs in the room, who gets resources, and who gets promoted. The reframing is not spin. It is a discipline that forces you to trace everything you do back to the metric it protects or moves. Start with the last three things you reported as accomplishments and ask what would have happened if you had not done them. That answer is your new talking point.

Avoid Becoming the AI Operator

When you develop genuine AI proficiency, people will start routing requests to you. That is a sign of trust and it feels like visibility, but it can quietly become a ceiling if you are not deliberate about how you respond to it. The trap is not the proficiency. It is what happens when the proficiency becomes your identity. The person who builds the system should not also be the person who maintains it indefinitely. One of those roles accumulates influence. The other accumulates tasks.

Consider a marketing operations manager who becomes the go-to person for AI-generated campaign briefs across five teams. At first it feels like leverage. She is consulted, visible, and seen as someone who can move fast. Six months later she is running the same workflow 40 times a month for different requesters, none of whom have learned to do it themselves, and she has no time left for the strategic work she was originally hired to do. The role did not change officially. It just quietly filled with execution that should have been distributed the moment it was documented.

The move that protects you is to treat every request as a documentation opportunity. When someone asks you to run a workflow, run it once and document how you did it. When someone asks you to build a prompt, build it and add it to a shared library with instructions.

When someone asks you to set up an automation, set it up and write the standard operating procedure before you hand it off. Every time you do this, you move from being the person who does the thing to being the person who built the system that does the thing. Those are not the same level of influence, and over time the difference compounds significantly.

The way most people say it: "I handle most of the AI stuff for the team. Everyone comes to me when they need a prompt or wants to automate something."

The way it should sound: "I built a shared prompt library and documented the automation workflows we use most often so the whole team can run them independently. I spend my time now identifying new opportunities where AI can reduce friction rather than maintaining the ones we have already solved. In the last quarter that freed up roughly six hours a week that I redirected toward campaign strategy."

Proximity to Decision Making

Getting closer to where decisions get made is a practical skill, not a political one, and it starts with a habit most people overlook. The professionals who consistently end up in the room where strategy gets set are not there because they were invited. They are there because they made themselves impossible to exclude by consistently surfacing the kind of observations that nobody else was bringing forward.

Consider a customer success manager who notices that accounts churning in months 7 through 9 all had the same onboarding experience in month 2. She has three options. She can file the observation in a note and move on. She can raise it as a complaint in a team meeting. Or she can bring it to her VP with the data attached, a clear articulation of the pattern, and a specific question about who owns the decision to change month 2 onboarding.

The first option disappears. The second option makes her sound like someone who finds problems. The third option makes her someone whose pattern recognition is worth paying attention to before decisions get made.

The sequence matters. Observation, evidence, ownership question. Not complaint, not recommendation, not solution. State the pattern clearly, attach the data that supports it, and ask who owns the decision about how to address it. That positions you as someone who thinks structurally rather than reactionally. Do it consistently across enough conversations and you will find yourself included in the discussions that happen before the meeting rather than during it.

The way most people say it: "I flagged that the handoff between onboarding and customer success wasn't working well."

The way it should sound: "I identified that accounts churning between months 7 and 9 shared a specific gap in their month 2 onboarding experience. I brought the pattern to our VP with three quarters of data attached and a recommendation for which team owns the fix. We are now piloting a change to the month 2 touchpoint for new accounts in that tier."

Reduce Replaceability

The most direct way to reduce your replaceability is to become the person who holds context that no single system captures. AI can generate analysis. It cannot hold the institutional memory of why a decision was made two years ago, what trade-off was accepted at the time, and why reversing it now would have consequences that do not show up in any dashboard. That knowledge lives with people, and the people who accumulate it across functions rather than within a single lane become genuinely difficult to replace.

Consider a senior project manager at a technology company who has worked across the product, engineering, and go-to-market teams over four years. When a new initiative launches that requires all three teams to align on a shared definition of done, she is the only person in the room who knows that engineering and product defined that term differently 18 months ago, that it caused a significant delay on the last major release, and that the go-to-market team was never told about the resolution. That context does not live in any project management tool. It lives in her, and the organization cannot function as well without it.

The practical way to build this kind of context deliberately is to schedule a 30-minute conversation once a month with someone in a department your work touches but that you do not regularly collaborate with. Ask them what is creating friction in their workflow and listen for the places where your team's outputs or timelines are part of the answer. Do that across three or four functions consistently and within a year you will hold a picture of how the organization actually works that very few people at any level can match.

The way most people say it: "I have been here long enough to know how things work across the different teams."

The way it should sound: "I meet regularly with counterparts in product, finance, and customer success to understand where their priorities are and where our team's work creates friction for them. That context has helped us avoid three significant cross-functional misalignments this year that would have cost us time and budget we did not have."

In an environment where AI can generate analysis faster than most teams can consume it, the scarcest skill is not producing insight. It is interpreting it clearly and being willing to state what it means. Most people stop at the data. They share the report, summarize the findings, and leave the room without saying what they think should happen next. That habit is costly, because the person who fills that silence consistently is the person who ends up shaping the direction.

Consider a revenue operations analyst who runs a monthly performance report for the sales leadership team. She has two options for how she closes that report. She can end with a summary of what the data showed, which is what most analysts do, or she can end with a recommendation based on what the data implies. The first version makes her a reliable reporter. The second version makes her an adviser. The difference in how leadership sees her role, and therefore what conversations they include her in, is significant and it compounds quickly.

The one sentence that changes everything is the implication sentence. Instead of closing with "Here is what the data shows," close with "Here is what I think we should do about it and here's why." That sentence requires taking a position and standing behind it, which is exactly why most people leave it out. The willingness to do it consistently, even when you turn out to be wrong sometimes, builds a kind of trust that no amount of accurate reporting can replicate.

The way most people say it: "I put together the monthly performance report and shared it with the leadership team."

The way it should sound: "I delivered the monthly performance report and included a recommendation. Two of the three initiatives we are tracking are underperforming for the same underlying reason, and I proposed consolidating them into a single effort with revised success metrics. The leadership team aligned on the recommendation and we are restructuring the initiatives going into next quarter."

Everything in this chapter points toward the same practical outcome. When you reframe your work around consequences, systematize what you know, build proximity to decisions, expand your contextual awareness, and own the interpretation of what the data means, you create capacity. The question is what you do with it.

The answer is not to fill it with more execution. The answer is to protect it deliberately for the work described in this chapter. The work that is most worth systematizing first is the work that is high volume, structurally repetitive, and currently consuming the hours that should be going toward interpretation, integration, and decision-level conversations.

Incident reports are one of the clearest examples. Most postmortems follow the same structure every single time. The same sections, the same stakeholder questions, the same language patterns for root-cause statements and remediation notes.

Yet teams rebuild them from scratch after every major event, spending hours on documentation that could be assembled automatically from the data sources that already exist. When you build a system that pulls from your incident ticketing tool, your monitoring dashboards, and your CRM to generate a complete audience-specific postmortem automatically, you do not just save time. You eliminate an entire category of reactive work that was consuming the hours you need for everything this chapter has described.

Customer onboarding operates the same way. Every new customer receives a welcome email, a setup guide, role-specific next steps, and a first-30-days success plan. The structure is identical every time. The personalization is minimal and mostly mechanical. When that journey gets systematized so that entering a few account details generates a complete onboarding sequence automatically, the time recovered goes back to the work that actually requires judgment. Understanding what the customer is trying to accomplish. Identifying where they are likely to stall. Being present in the conversations that determine whether they renew or leave.

The pattern across both examples is the same. Identify the work that is structurally repetitive. Separate what is fixed from what is patterned from what is genuinely unique. Systematize the first two. Protect the third for human judgment. Then take the hours that come back and put them somewhere they compound.

That is what getting your time back actually means. Not working fewer hours. Working in the hours you recover on the things that compound. The 85–90 percent of time you have with your kids before they turn 18 does not expand because you worked harder. It expands because you built systems that stopped consuming it, and then you protected what came back.

Chapter 8

Spending Time on What Actually Matters

Roughly 85–90 percent of the in-person time you will ever spend with your children happens before they turn 18. Most parents learn that statistic too late, somewhere in the middle of a stretch of years that felt busy and necessary and like it would eventually slow down. It does not slow down on its own. You have to decide to slow it down, and that decision requires having something to slow it down with. Time is not freed by wanting it back. It is freed by building systems that stop consuming it.

Before any of the sections in this chapter will move the needle, one thing has to change first. What you do matters, but how you communicate what you do matters significantly more. Most professionals are doing more valuable work than the people around them realize, not because the work is hidden, but because the language used to describe it undersells it.

The difference between being seen as an executor and being seen as a strategic contributor is rarely the work itself. It is the sentence used to describe it in a meeting, a performance review, or a conversation with a decision maker. Each section in this chapter includes an example of how most people currently talk about that area of their work, and how that same contribution sounds when the language reflects its actual impact.

AI Parenting Paradox

This book is about using AI to get your time back. The whole premise is that the right tools, used with intention, can return hours to your week that you can spend on the things that actually matter. And if you are a parent, those things are not abstract. They are a kid who needs help with homework. A partner you have not had a real conversation with since Tuesday. A version of yourself that existed before you started running at this pace and somewhere along the way forgot to stop.

But here is the part that would be dishonest to skip over. The people most likely to be experimenting with AI right now are not parents. They are not the ones up at 11 p.m. finishing the mental checklist of everything that did not get done. They are not the ones squeezing work into the margins of a school pickup and a dinner that nobody ate and a bedtime that took 45 minutes longer than it should have. The early adopters, the people building workflows and testing tools and talking about their AI productivity gains, are largely younger, less encumbered, and working in environments that give them the space to experiment.

Parents, statistically, are watching from the outside. That matters. Not because parents are behind and need to catch up. But because the gap between who needs AI the most and who is actually using it is not a technology gap. It is not a skills gap. It is something closer to a capacity gap. When every hour is already spoken for, picking up something new, even something that promises to give you hours back, can feel like one more thing you do not have room for. The very condition AI is designed to solve is the same condition that makes it hardest to start.

I want to name that contradiction clearly because I think a lot of parents have picked up books like this one, read about frameworks and tools and time-saving systems, and felt a quiet frustration that never quite made it onto the page. The frustration of being told the solution exists while feeling completely unable to reach it.

This chapter is about closing that gap. Not with a longer to-do list. Not with a better system on top of an already full life. But by making the case, with real evidence, that the path from where you are right now to the life you actually want is shorter than it feels. And that the first step is not a tool. It is a decision.

Why Parents Are Getting Left Behind

If you look at the data on who is actually using AI right now, a picture emerges quickly. The current profile of a regular AI user is younger, more likely to work in tech or finance, more likely to live in a city, and more likely to have an employer actively encouraging them to experiment.

According to a 2025 Pew Research Center survey,[1] workers ages 18–29 are the most likely of any age group to use AI chatbots at work at least a few times a month, while usage drops steadily among workers in their 30s, 40s, 50s, and 60s. Complementary 2025 adoption analyses[2] find that Gen X and Baby Boomers together make up roughly two-thirds of all non-users of generative AI tools, even though many of them are in peak caregiving and career years.

Now think about who that profile leaves out:

- The parent of a seven-year-old who is also managing a full-time job, a household, and a schedule that was already at capacity before anyone added anything new to it

---

[1]Pew Research Center. "About 1 in 5 U.S. workers now use AI in their job, up since last year." 2025. `www.pewresearch.org/short-reads/2025/10/06/about-1-in-5-us-workers-now-use-ai-in-their-job-up-since-last-year`

[2]"The State of Generative AI Adoption in 2025." 2025. `www.stlouisfed.org/on-the-economy/2025/nov/state-generative-ai-adoption-2025`

- The working mother who, according to a 2024 University of Bath study[3] of 3,000 parents, is carrying 71 percent of all household mental load tasks on top of everything else
- The father who, according to KPMG's Working Parents Survey,[4] is watching his partner report lower satisfaction with her personal well-being and her time with family than any other group tracked in the research
- The parent who read the first chapter of this book at 11 p.m. because that was the only quiet hour available.

These are not people who are unaware that AI exists. They are people who are too underwater to surface long enough to try it.

The 2025 Northwestern University study[5] of 416 employed parents put a name to this problem. Researchers found that parents working the longest hours and facing the most daily pressure were the least likely to adopt AI tools. The gap was not about access; it was not about education or income or technical ability. It was about trust and mental space, specifically the absence of both.

The researchers described AI adoption as depending on three things: the mental room to explore and confirm a tool actually works, the feeling of safety to let it play a role at home, and a sense of control over how it is used. When any one of those three things is missing, adoption stalls. When all three are depleted, which is the baseline state for most overwhelmed parents, the tools sit untouched.

---

[3]www.bath.ac.uk/announcements/mothers-bear-the-brunt-of-the-mental-load-managing-7-in-10-household-tasks

[4]https://kpmg.com/us/en/media/news/kpmg-working-parents-survey-2025.html

[5]www.medill.northwestern.edu/news/2025/research-suggests-less-busy-parents-use-ai-more-but-they-may-not-trust-it.html

They named this the AI Parenting Paradox. Parents with more available time were four times more likely to trust and actually use AI than parents who were completely maxed out. Four times. The people with the least to lose from trying something new were the ones doing all the trying, and the people with the most to gain were the ones staying put.

I get it. If someone told me they could potentially give me more time back to spend with my family, I would be too tired to believe them. This is usually where I encourage people that the Internet is your friend. If you doubt it, go do the research. So here is your research.

The Gallup and Walton Family Foundation study of more than 2,200 teachers found that the ones who did reach for AI tools, who used them at least once a week, saved nearly six hours every week. Six hours that they put back into writing more personal notes, giving more attention to the kids in front of them, and getting home earlier. To their own families. To themselves.

So how do we go from reading about the success of others getting their time back to seeing that outcome for ourselves? Trust-building exercises. Low stakes, still meaningful, and nothing that takes more than five minutes because we know you do not have that long anyway.

Take a photo of your fridge and ask ChatGPT to suggest five dinners you can make with what you already have. That's it. No grocery list to write, no recipe sites to scroll through, no decision fatigue about what to cook while a kid is pulling on your sleeve. You get five options in seconds and you pick one. That is four minutes of your evening returned, and more importantly, that is your first proof of concept. You asked, it answered, it helped. Trust just moved one notch forward.

Or this one: Ask ChatGPT to generate a custom coloring page your child will love. Describe their favorite characters, their current obsession, whatever it is this week. A printable page lands in your hands in under a minute. On Saturday morning, while they color, you get 10 minutes that belong to you. Ten minutes of coffee while it is still hot. Ten minutes of quiet. Ten minutes that did not exist before you tried one small thing.

A 2025 study of 416 employed parents found that AI adoption in families is driven less by access and more by trust. Parents who feel confident that AI is competent, benevolent, and under their control are several times more likely to use it with their children.

The proof is in the pudding. If we want to change these numbers and put these tools back in the hands of parents, we have to participate in exercises that build that trust one small win at a time. Here are 10 more ideas. Pick one. Start it this week. Then take count of what you were able to get back as a result.

1. The full mental dump. Paste everything in your head, school emails, appointments, half-finished to-do lists, into a chat and ask AI to turn it into an organized, dated checklist or calendar entries. Get the noise out of your brain and onto a page in under three minutes.

2. The seven-day meal plan. Paste what is in your fridge and pantry and ask for a full week of family dinners with a grocery list, a budget cap, and swaps for picky eaters. One prompt, one week handled.

3. The parenting script. Ask AI to draft age-appropriate language for the hard conversations. Meltdowns, sibling conflict, bedtime battles, talking about scary news. Get a script, then adjust it until it sounds like you. Having the words ready before you need them changes everything.

4. The bedtime story series. Have AI co-write a bedtime story starring your child, their favorite characters, or a place your family is traveling to next. Build it into a series. Reuse it. Let it become theirs.

5. The school admin offload. Use AI to summarize long school newsletters, draft emails to teachers and coaches, fill in forms before you review them, and build packing lists for camps or trips. All the administrative friction of parenting, handled in a fraction of the time.

6. The calendar guardian. Connect an AI assistant to your calendar and ask it to flag conflicts, suggest carpool options, and block family time or personal time before work fills every open gap. Protect the hours before they disappear.

7. The homework helper. Use kid-friendly AI tools to explain assignments in simpler language, generate practice questions, or turn a topic into something creative. A comic about photosynthesis. A quiz about fractions. Learning that does not feel like pulling teeth.

8. The celebration planner. Offload the mental load of birthdays, holidays, weekend activities, and small daily moments. Ten-minute games for after dinner. A theme for Saturday. An activity that costs nothing. Let AI carry the planning so you can just show up.

9. The pressure valve. Use AI as a private place to vent. Name what you are feeling, describe what happened, and ask for a reframe or a quick coping strategy. It is not therapy. But it is available at 11 p.m. when nothing else is, and sometimes that is enough.

10. The decision helper. Ask AI to map the pros, cons, and long-term impact of a choice you are sitting with. Switching daycares. Saying yes to a work trip. Adding one more activity to an already full schedule. Think out loud with something that will actually think back.

One of these is the right starting point for where you are right now. You do not need to do all 10. You do not need to do them in order. You just need to start somewhere small enough to actually try, notice what comes back to you when you do, and let that be enough proof to take one more step.

The Lesson They're Already Learning

My son did not need a lesson. He needed to know how many minutes until his dad came home with ice cream. It was a completely ordinary evening, and my husband had run out to pick up a treat for us. My son asked me when dad would be back, and I told him I was not sure. He asked again. Then again.

By the fifth time, I was out of patient answers, so I pulled up the maps app on my phone that showed my husband's location through contact sharing. I was not thinking about teaching anything. I was thinking about ending the loop of questions long enough to get five minutes of peace.

When the screen came up, there was a small blue dot moving slowly down a road, and my son went completely still. He stared at it. Then he asked, "How many minutes is that?" I looked at the distance and told him it showed 4.2 miles, but that I was not sure exactly how long that would take.

So I did the only natural thing in that moment and said I would ask AI to figure it out. That was it. One moment. I did not plan it, explain it, or frame it as a learning opportunity. I just solved a problem in front of him the way I normally would.

Now, whenever my son has a question he cannot answer on his own, he asks me to ask AI. If I already know the answer, that satisfies him completely. But when I cannot answer him, he has learned through one unplanned moment that there are other resources that can answer his questions quickly and that going to find an answer is always an option. He did not learn that from a conversation I had with him about the value of curiosity. He learned it by watching me refuse to let "I don't know" be the end of the story.

Your kids are not waiting for you to sit them down and explain how the world works. They are studying you right now, in the ordinary moments you probably do not think of as teaching moments at all. The way you respond when something breaks. The way you handle a question you cannot answer. The way you keep trying when you are frustrated and the solution still has not shown up. Every one of those moments is a lesson, and your children are taking notes whether you realize it or not.

This is not a new idea. Psychologist Albert Bandura[6] spent decades documenting what he called observational learning, which is the process by which children absorb behaviors, attitudes, and problem-solving approaches simply by watching the people closest to them.

His research showed that children pay attention not just to what adults do, but to the intention behind what they do. They are not passive observers sitting in the background. They are functioning like scientists, forming hypotheses about how the world works based on the evidence you give them every single day.

The question is not whether your kids are learning from you. They are. The only real question is what, exactly, they are picking up.

The Signal They're Actually Reading

When you hit a wall and your first instinct is to stop, your children learn that walls are where effort ends. When you hit a wall and your first instinct is to find another way in, they learn that walls are just the beginning of the process. This distinction quietly shapes how they approach difficulty for the rest of their lives. Not the conversation

---

[6] https://hr.berkeley.edu/grow/grow-your-community/wisdom-caf%C3%A9-wednesday/how-social-learning-theory-works

you have about it later when things have calmed down. The moment itself is what registers.

Research from Zero to Three[7] confirms that the single most powerful thing a parent can do to build curiosity in a child is to model it themselves. Not explain it. Not encourage it with praise. Model it by doing it in front of them. Children who regularly watch adults ask questions, explore options, and stay engaged with a problem develop stronger curiosity of their own, and that curiosity connects directly to better academic performance in reading and math once they enter school. The modeling comes first. The outcomes follow.

This is exactly where AI tools enter the picture in a way most parents have not considered yet. When you open a tool to help you find an answer, you are not just solving a problem for yourself. You are demonstrating a behavior to the people watching you. You are showing your child what it looks like to seek out resources rather than give up or pretend to already know something you do not. You are showing them that not knowing something is not a dead end. It is a starting point, and starting points are where the real work begins.

The Difference Between Using a Tool and Modeling One

There is a version of using AI tools that teaches your kids nothing useful, and it is the version most of us default to without thinking. That version looks like this: You disappear into your phone, get an answer, move on. The tool is invisible. The process is invisible. Your child sees a parent staring at a screen, which is the same thing they see dozens of times a day, and walks away with no new information about how to think or how problems get solved.

---

[7] www.zerotothree.org/resource/nurturing-your-young-childs-curiosity

There is another version entirely, and it looks different from the very first moment. That version begins when your child asks you something you do not know, and instead of guessing or brushing it off, you say, "I don't know. Let's figure it out together." You sit down with them. You think out loud about how to phrase the question in a way that will get useful results. You look at what comes back and you talk through it in terms they can follow.

Maybe you push further because the first answer raised more questions. Maybe you find out the initial result was incomplete or needed some context to make sense. Maybe you both get curious about something you did not expect to find.

That second version teaches an entirely different set of skills. It teaches that questions are worth pursuing all the way to an answer. It teaches that tools exist to help you think more clearly, not to replace the thinking you need to do yourself. It teaches that the process of finding an answer carries as much value as the answer itself.

MIT researchers[8] studying parent-child learning interactions found that conventional approaches, where the adult already has the answer and simply delivers it, build basic skills in the short run but often fail to develop complex problem-solving abilities over time. The interactions that build lasting capability are the ones centered on genuine inquiry and open exploration. When you model how to use a search or AI tool with intention, you are giving your child exactly that kind of interaction.

What AI Literacy Actually Looks Like at Home

AI literacy is not a class your child takes at school or a program you sign them up for on the weekend. It is a posture toward information that gets built through repeated exposure to how the adults around

[8]https://news.mit.edu/2022/research-collaboration-to-examine-parent-child-learning-interactions-0110

them handle not knowing things. The formal curriculum will catch up eventually, but the habits form now, in your kitchen, on your couch, in the car when someone asks a question that nobody in the vehicle can answer from memory.

Here is what it looks like in practice. Your child asks why the sky turns red at sunset. You could guess. You could offer something that sounds plausible and move on. Or you could say, "That's actually a really interesting question. I think it has something to do with the way light travels through the atmosphere, but I want to make sure I get this right. Let me show you how I'd look it up."

Then you do it together. You ask the question out loud before you type it, so they can hear how you frame it. You look at what comes back and explain what you are reading in terms they can understand. You let them ask a follow-up question and you model how to pursue that one too, going through the same process again without making it feel like a chore.

A meta-analysis of 88 studies[9] on digital parenting published in 2025 found that parents who actively use technology alongside their children—what researchers call co-use—produce the most positive outcomes in their children's relationship with digital tools. Not restriction alone. Not unlimited access without guidance. Active, shared use where the parent stays present and engaged in the process. Co-use had the largest protective effect of any digital parenting strategy measured across all 88 studies. You do not have to be a technology expert to do this. You just have to be willing to be uncertain alongside your child instead of pretending a confidence you do not actually have.

If you treat AI tools with visible anxiety, dismissal, or contempt, you are modeling that response too. If you say things like "I don't trust any of that" or "I have no idea how this stuff works" in a tone

---

[9]www.sciencedirect.com/science/article/pii/S1747938X25000363

that closes the door rather than opens it, your child absorbs that posture as the right one to have.

They learn that new tools are threatening rather than useful. They learn that confusion is something to be ashamed of rather than something to work through. They learn that the appropriate response to technological change is to opt out and wait for someone else to figure it out first.

That is a costly inheritance in a world where the people who know how to work alongside these tools will have a meaningful advantage over those who do not.

Research[10] on digital parenting found that parents who demonstrate what researchers call efficient usage—meaning they actively leverage technology as a tool for growth and learning rather than something to be managed or feared—raised children who were significantly less likely to develop problematic relationships with technology over time.

The parent's visible approach to the tool shaped the child's relationship with it, and that relationship transferred in measurable ways. You do not have to love every new tool that arrives or present yourself as an enthusiast for things you are still figuring out. But the way you visibly process the learning curve around technology will either give your children permission to struggle productively with new and unfamiliar things, or it will teach them to avoid that discomfort entirely. One of those responses will serve them throughout their lives. The other will not.

The most useful thing you can do right now is not to find the perfect educational AI application or set up a structured learning session with your kids on a Saturday morning. It is to stop making your own thinking process invisible when you are working through a problem in front of them.

---

[10]https://pmc.ncbi.nlm.nih.gov/articles/PMC11799820/

When you use a tool to find an answer, say out loud what you are doing and why. When you are unsure how to phrase a question to get useful results, think through it out loud so they can hear your reasoning. When the first result is not quite what you needed, let your child see you try again with different words and a different angle. When you find something genuinely useful, take a moment to explain what made it useful and what you did to track it down. These are the small moments that stack into actual capability over time, and they cost you almost nothing to share.

Everyone Starts as a Beginner

Think back to the ice cream story for a moment. My son did not need a manual. He did not need a structured training session or a scheduled time to sit down and learn. He needed to watch someone he trusted use a tool to solve a real problem that mattered to him in that moment, and the rest happened on its own. One unplanned demonstration, and now he reaches for AI the way most kids reach for Google.

The new hire sitting across from you on their first day is not so different from that little boy watching a blue dot move down a road toward ice cream. They are in an unfamiliar environment, trying to make sense of how things work around here, and they are watching you far more carefully than you realize.

They are reading your habits, your shortcuts, your instincts, and your relationship with the tools you use every day. They are forming their understanding of what good looks like in this role by studying the person who already occupies it. Whether you intend to teach them or not, you are teaching them something. The question, again, is what exactly they are picking up.

Chapter 9

AI Solutions for Employees

The first 90 days of a new hire's time at your company are not just an adjustment period. They are the highest-leverage window you will ever have with that employee. Research from the Society for Human Resource Management[1] found that effective onboarding improves new hire retention by 82 percent and productivity by 70 percent. Those numbers do not come from better paperwork or faster system access. They come from whether the new employee feels seen, supported, and shown what success looks like in practice.

Most managers understand this at some level. What fewer managers understand is that the way they personally model AI tools during those first 90 days will shape how that employee uses them, avoids them, or fears them for the rest of their time at the company. Onboarding is the first moment when organizations can demonstrate how AI supports the way work gets done. If the manager never opens a tool in front of the new hire, never thinks out loud about how they find answers, and never shows the process behind the output, the new hire draws their own conclusions. They either assume they are supposed to already know everything, or they assume that the tools are not really meant for them yet. Both conclusions are wrong, and both are expensive.

---

[1] https://lifthcm.com/article/employee-onboarding-best-practices-guide

What Beginners Actually Need

A beginner does not need perfection modeled for them. A beginner needs to see that not knowing something is survivable, and that there are reliable ways to close the gap between what you know and what the situation requires. This is true at age 6 and it is true at age 36.

The emotional experience of being new at something does not change very much with age. The discomfort of not knowing where things are, how decisions get made, and what the unwritten rules look like is the same for a child starting at a new school and an experienced professional starting a new role.

What changes is the expectation. Children are generally given permission to not know things yet. New hires often are not, even when they should be. The pressure to perform quickly, to ask the right questions without asking too many, and to appear competent before they have had any real chance to become competent creates a quiet anxiety that most onboarding processes do not address.

The first weeks in a role are when employees need structure and direction. They are learning new systems, adjusting to workflows, and finding out how their role connects to what the organization is actually trying to accomplish. Without clear guidance, introducing AI at this stage can confuse rather than support.

This is where the manager's behavior matters more than any onboarding tool or training module. When a manager thinks out loud in front of a new hire, when they say, "I'm not sure how to pull that data; let me show you how I'd look it up," they accomplish far more than solving the immediate problem. They are handing the new hire something that no job description, onboarding portal, or training deck ever captures. They are showing them how a problem gets defined in this environment, how it gets prioritized, and what the thinking looks like before a tool ever enters the picture.

That sequence matters more than most managers realize. When a new hire watches their manager stop, name what the problem is, talk through how they are approaching it, and then reach for a specific tool to move faster toward a resolution, they are not just learning about the tool. They are learning the manager's mental framework for what counts as a problem worth solving, what a solution is supposed to look like, and which resources are trusted enough to help get there. That is institutional knowledge that used to take years to absorb through proximity and repetition. A manager who makes that process visible and audible in the first 90 days compresses that transfer dramatically.

The new hire who watches you work through a problem out loud and then sees you use AI to accelerate the back half of it will eventually do the same thing on their own. They will frame problems the way you frame them. They will know which questions to ask before reaching for a tool because they watched you ask those questions first. They will understand that AI is not the starting point of good thinking but the accelerant that comes after the thinking has already begun. That understanding is not something you can put in a training module. It is something you demonstrate, in real moments, with real stakes, the same way every meaningful skill has ever been passed from one person to another.

If your organization uses ChatGPT, the first feature you should introduce to a new hire within their first 90 days is a *project*. A project inside ChatGPT is a dedicated workspace where conversations, uploaded files, and custom instructions live together in one place rather than scattered across unrelated chat threads. When you set one up with a new hire around their actual role, you are not just showing them a feature. You are showing them how to organize their thinking inside a tool so that the tool gets smarter and more useful over time rather than starting from scratch every single session.

Let's look at three examples of what a meaningful project looks like in practice. Any of them can be adapted regardless of what function the new hire is stepping into.

The first example is a project built around the new hire's first real assignment. Name it after the actual work in front of them, something like "Q3 Client Launch" or "New Territory Ramp" or "90-Day Integration." Upload two or three documents they will reference during that assignment, such as a product one-pager, a recent internal report, or a team communication template. Then set a custom instruction that reflects something true about how their role communicates—for example: "Responses should be concise, professional, and written for a business audience that values clarity over detail." That instruction does not need to be perfect on day 1. It just needs to reflect something real, and it can be refined as the new hire settles into the role. The point is that by the end of the first week they have a workspace that already knows something about their job, rather than a blank screen asking them to start from nothing every time.

The second example is a project built around a recurring deliverable. If the new hire will be responsible for a weekly report, a standing client update, or a regular internal summary, build the project around that output. Upload a strong example of what a finished version looks like. Add any background context about the audience, the format the team expects, and the level of detail that is appropriate. A custom instruction here might say something like "This project is for drafting weekly status updates. Responses should be written in a direct, informative tone and should lead with outcomes before explaining process." Every time the new hire opens this project to work on that deliverable, the tool is already oriented to the task without them having to explain the context from scratch.

The third example is a project built around learning the business. New hires spend an enormous amount of cognitive energy in their first 90 days just trying to understand the landscape, the terminology, the competitive environment, and the internal language of how things get discussed. A project loaded with company materials, team glossaries, recent strategy documents, or competitive summaries gives the new hire a place to ask questions and process information without feeling like they are taking up someone else's time every time they need to understand something. A custom instruction for this project might say, "You are helping a new team member understand our business. Explain things clearly, define any industry terms that come up, and connect information back to how it affects their role." This kind of project does not replace human mentorship—it supplements it, and it is available at 10:00 p.m. when the new hire is still trying to make sense of everything they absorbed during their first week.

If your organization uses Microsoft Copilot, the equivalent starting point is a saved prompt inside a notebook. A notebook in Copilot holds longer context than a standard prompt window, which means it can carry the background information, tone guidance, and role-specific framing that a new hire would otherwise have to explain every single session. Sitting down with a new hire to build their first saved notebook prompt is one of the most practical 30 minutes a manager can spend during onboarding.

The Copilot equivalent works the same way, and there are three notebook prompt examples worth walking through so that the concept becomes tangible rather than abstract.

The first is a saved prompt built around the recurring task the new hire will do most often in their first month. If they will be summarizing meeting notes, the notebook prompt might include the format the team expects, the level of detail that is appropriate, and any standing context about the project or client those meetings relate to. A prompt like this might read, "I attend weekly alignment calls for a client implementation project. After each call, I need to produce a summary that includes decisions made, open items with owners, and any risks flagged. The audience is internal and the tone should be direct and action-oriented." That is not a complicated prompt. It is just clear thinking written down in advance, and every time the new hire opens that notebook they are starting from context rather than from zero.

The second is a saved prompt built around drafting internal communications. New hires spend more time than anyone expects trying to figure out how to write inside a new organization, what level of formality is appropriate, how much background to provide, and whose name should appear at the top of an update. A notebook prompt that carries the company's voice guidelines, the new hire's role context, and a few examples of what strong internal communication looks like gives the tool enough information to produce a useful first draft rather than a generic one. The new hire still edits it. The prompt just removes the paralysis of the blank page in an environment where they are still learning the unwritten rules.

The third is a saved prompt built around preparing for conversations. One of the most anxiety-producing parts of being new in a role is walking into meetings, one-on-ones, or client calls without enough context to contribute meaningfully. A notebook prompt that helps a new hire prepare for a recurring meeting type—by pulling together relevant background, surfacing the right questions to ask, and framing the conversation around what a successful outcome looks like—gives them a repeatable way to show up prepared rather than hoping they absorbed enough from the week before. A prompt here might say, "Help me prepare for a weekly check-in with my manager. I want to come in with a clear update on my priorities, one or two questions I need input on, and any blockers I should flag. Keep the format brief and conversational." That prompt does not change much week to week. But the new hire who has it available will consistently show up to those conversations better prepared than the one who does not.

In both cases, the goal is the same. You are not introducing a feature. You are introducing a habit, the habit of setting up a tool to work for a specific person doing a specific job rather than treating every session like the first one. A new hire who leaves their first 90 days with a working project or a saved notebook prompt has something most tenured employees do not have: a tool that already knows something about them and is ready to help them move faster because of it.

Use Cases: 10 Ways to Put Projects and Notebooks to Work

The three examples in the previous section were meant to get you started. This section goes deeper. Whether your organization runs on ChatGPT or Microsoft Copilot, the following 10 use cases give you and your new hire a concrete starting point for building a tool that reflects how their role works rather than how a generic demo suggests it might.

None of these require technical knowledge to set up. Each one requires about 30 minutes of intentional time between a manager and a new hire, and that investment will return itself many times over across the first 90 days and beyond.

Every organization has its own language, and new hires spend an enormous amount of energy in their first weeks pretending to understand it. Acronyms, internal shorthand, legacy project names, and process documentation written for people who already know the context all create a quiet tax on a new hire's attention that most managers never see.

These 10 use cases are not a checklist to complete; they are a menu to pull from based on what your new hire needs most in the moment they are in. One well-built project or notebook prompt set up in the first two weeks will do more for a new hire's confidence and capability than a stack of onboarding documents they will never return to.

The goal is not to give them everything at once. The goal is to show them that the tools available to them are already oriented toward their success and that someone took the time to set this up that way before they ever arrived.

Use Case 1: Decode Acronyms and Internal Docs

Set up a saved prompt or project instruction called "Onboarding Translator" with the following guidance loaded in:

> When I paste an internal message or document, explain the key points in plain language, define any acronyms, and list three follow-up questions I could ask to clarify expectations.

The new hire can then paste any confusing thread, policy snippet, or department update directly into the tool and get a plain-language translation back in seconds.

They stop falling behind in meetings because they missed a reference from six months ago, and they stop spending 30 minutes building up the courage to ask a colleague what something means. The tool absorbs those questions so the new hire can save their face time for conversations that actually matter.

Use Case 2: Generate a 30-60-90 Day Plan

Most new hires receive a vague sense of what success looks like in their first 90 days. A few receive a formal plan. Almost none receive something they actually built themselves with enough specificity to hold onto when the first week gets overwhelming and priorities blur together.

Set up a saved prompt or project called "30-60-90 Ramp Plan" with the following guidance:

> Given this job description, org chart, and current project list, design a realistic 30-60-90 day plan with weekly learning goals, key relationships to build, and quick-win tasks I can accomplish in the first 30 days.

Have the new hire paste in their job description and whatever context they have been given about the team. Let the tool draft a plan, then sit down together and refine it into something real. The value is not just the document that comes out; it is the conversation the document forces, where the new hire tells you what feels unclear and you fill in the gaps that no onboarding checklist ever captures.

Use Case 3: Map Key People and Questions

New hires know they need to build relationships. What most of them do not know is who exactly those people are, what those people own, and what a useful first conversation with each of them sounds like. Without a map, early networking becomes either random or anxiety-producing, and the new hire ends up having surface-level conversations that do not build the context they need.

Set up a saved prompt or project called "Relationship Map" with the following guidance:

> Using this team or department description, identify the 10 most important people I should build relationships with in my first 90 days, explain what each person owns and how their work connects to mine, and suggest two or three specific questions I could ask each of them in a first one-on-one.

Have the new hire paste in whatever org information they have been given. The output gives them a starting list they can prioritize with you, and the suggested questions give them a way into early conversations that is specific enough to be genuinely useful rather than generically polite.

Use Case 4: Daily Standup and Reflection Buddy

The cognitive load of the first 90 days is real, and it compounds. New hires absorb an enormous amount of information each day, and without a consistent place to process it, the questions pile up, the open items get lost, and the learning slows down faster than anyone realizes.

Set up a saved prompt or project called "Daily Check-In" with the following guidance:

> Each morning, help me turn my notes from the day before into a focused three-bullet plan covering what I need to learn today, what I need to execute, and one relationship I should invest in. Each afternoon, help me summarize what I accomplished, what I learned, and what questions I need to bring to my manager or a colleague tomorrow.

This use case does not require the manager at all once it is set up. The new hire runs it on their own, and within two weeks they have a running log of their own ramp that makes every one-on-one with you more focused and more productive because they are showing up with specific questions instead of a vague sense of how things are going.

Use Case 5: Explain Systems and Workflows

Every role comes with tools and workflows the new hire has never seen before, and formal training rarely arrives at the exact moment the new hire needs it. The gap between when they encounter a system and when someone has time to walk them through it is where confusion becomes frustration and frustration becomes disengagement.

Set up a saved prompt or project called "Workflow Explainer" with the following guidance:

> When I paste a description or screenshot of a workflow, tool, or process, explain what it does, describe how my role interacts with it, and give me a three-step practice exercise I can do on my own to get comfortable before I need to use it in a real situation.

This prompt turns every system the new hire encounters into a self-guided learning moment. They do not have to wait for a training session to get oriented, and they do not have to pull a tenured colleague away from their own work every time a new tool appears on their screen.

Use Case 6: Prepare for and Debrief Meetings

Meetings are where culture lives in most organizations, and new hires are at a significant disadvantage in them. They do not know the history behind the agenda items. They do not know which questions are safe to ask out loud and which ones belong in a follow-up conversation. They do not always catch what was decided versus what was just discussed.

Set up a saved prompt or project called "Meeting Prep and Recap" with the following guidance:

> Before a meeting, summarize the agenda and any background notes I provide, suggest three questions I should consider asking, and highlight the decisions that are likely to be made so I know what to listen for. After the

> meeting, take my raw notes and turn them into clear action items with owners and deadlines.

This use case earns its value every single week of the new hire's ramp. They show up to meetings more prepared, they leave with cleaner next steps, and they start building the reputation of someone who follows through, which is the reputation that matters most in the first 90 days.

Use Case 7: Simplify Policies and Benefits

HR handbooks and benefits documents are written by people who understand them for people who are supposed to read them carefully. New hires rarely do either, and the result is missed enrollment deadlines, misunderstood policies, and avoidable confusion that creates friction between the new hire and HR at exactly the moment when that relationship should be easy.

Set up a saved prompt or project called "HR Handbook Guide" with the following guidance:

> When I paste a policy or benefits document, summarize only the sections that are most relevant to my role and situation, highlight any decisions I need to make and the deadlines attached to them, and suggest two or three questions I should confirm directly with HR before I assume I understand correctly.

This prompt does not replace HR. It prepares the new hire to have a better conversation with HR by the time they get there, which saves time on both sides and reduces the chance that something important slips through the gap between a long document and a distracted first week.

Use Case 8: Build a Focused Learning Path

Most organizations give new hires access to a wiki, a shared drive, a learning management system, or some combination of all three. Almost none of those resources are organized in a way that tells a new hire what to read first, what to read next, and what they can safely skip until later. The result is either overwhelm or avoidance, and neither one produces a new hire who is ramping up the way they should be.

Set up a saved prompt or project called "Learning Path Designer" with the following guidance:

> Given my role, my current experience level, and this list of internal resources, design a four-week learning path that tells me specifically what to read, watch, or practice each week and that explains why each item matters for how I will do my job.

Have the new hire paste in whatever resource list they have been given. The output is a prioritized sequence rather than a pile, and a new hire with a sequence is a new hire who makes progress rather than one who spends their third week still unsure where to start.

Use Case 9: Turn Feedback Into a Coaching Engine

Most new hires receive sporadic feedback in their first 90 days. A comment surfaces in a one-on-one. A note appears in a shared document. A passing remark lands after a meeting and then disappears before the new hire has had a chance to do anything with it.

Almost none of that feedback gets captured systematically or turned into an actionable development plan. The result is that patterns take months to surface and the new hire keeps relearning the same lesson in different contexts without ever realizing they are doing it.

Set up a saved prompt or project called "Feedback to Growth Plan" with the following guidance:

> When I paste feedback I have received from emails or conversations or document comments, extract the concrete behaviors being mentioned and group them into themes and then suggest one or two specific experiments I can run over the next week to practice improving in each theme. Have the new hire paste in snippets of feedback as they receive them throughout the ramp-up period.

Over time the tool turns scattered and disconnected comments into a living coaching map that the new hire owns. They can walk into a one-on-one and tell their manager exactly which themes they are working on and what they are trying that week. That kind of ownership signals maturity and self-awareness, and it shortens the path from receiving feedback to changing behavior in ways that make the manager's job meaningfully easier.

Use Case 10: Shadow the Role You Want, Not Just the One You Have

New hires are usually brought in to fill a clearly scoped role, and most of their attention in the first 90 days goes toward mastering that scope. The people who grow fastest, though, are the ones who quietly begin learning the next role while they are still building competence in their current one.

Most organizations do not have a formal path for this kind of stretch learning. The new hire sees their own ticket queue and their own project list and has no structured way to understand how more senior teammates are thinking about the same problems at a higher level of complexity and judgment.

Set up a saved prompt or project called "Role Shadowing Guide" with the following guidance:

> When I paste examples of work from more senior teammates such as strategy documents or project plans or meeting notes, analyze how that work differs from mine and identify the specific skills or judgment being applied that I am not yet demonstrating. Then suggest one concrete way I could practice that skill within my current scope this week.

Ask the new hire to collect real artifacts from people one level above them and run those artifacts through this guide on a regular basis. The tool makes the invisible gap between roles explicit and turns it into concrete weekly experiments. Instead of being told to think more strategically without any real sense of what that means in practice, the new hire can see examples of more senior thinking side by side with their own work and walk away with a specific thing to try rather than a vague aspiration to be better.

Agentic Solutions for Junior and Senior Employees

Projects and saved prompts are powerful starting points. But there is a next level of AI capability that most employees at every level have not touched yet and that every organization will be navigating in the next few years whether they plan for it or not. That next level is agents.

An AI agent is not a prompt you write and a response you read. An agent is a system that can plan a sequence of steps and take action across tools and data sources to complete a task with minimal back and forth from you. Where a prompt gives you a draft and waits for your next move, an agent can move on its own: pulling information, making decisions within a defined boundary, routing outputs to the right place, and surfacing only the moments that require a human in the loop.

Newer employees tend to embrace agents faster than tenured ones because the agent guides them through processes they are still learning, which makes the job easier from the start. More tenured employees sometimes resist because the agent changes the muscle memory they have already built.

Both groups need a bridge into this technology, and that bridge looks different depending on where they stand. The following use cases are organized by platform and written for both ends of the experience spectrum so that every employee has a concrete place to begin.

Copilot Studio Work IQ Coach for Power Users (Microsoft)

Senior employees are often the last to receive meaningful training with new tools because organizations assume their tenure compensates for their unfamiliarity. The most common result is that they use Copilot at 10 percent of its actual capacity while the junior employees around them move faster and faster with the same tools. This agent closes that gap without requiring anyone to sit through a training session that was not built for their role or their real work.

Use Case

Help mid-level and senior employees quietly level up their Copilot and Microsoft 365 skills so they are not being outpaced by the junior employees they manage.

How to Set It Up

Open your browser and go to `http://copilotstudio.microsoft.com`. Sign in with your Microsoft 365 work account. Once you are inside Copilot Studio, you will land on the home screen, where you will see a button in the upper left that says Create. Click that and select New Agent. Give the agent a name like "Work IQ Coach," and in the description field write something like: **This agent monitors my Microsoft 365 activity and suggests specific Copilot prompts tied to my actual documents, meetings, and deliverables**.

In the Instructions field, which is the core of how your agent behaves, write the following guidance:

> *Monitor this user's activity across Word, Excel, PowerPoint, and Teams. When you detect a recurring document type or deliverable, surface a specific Copilot prompt the user can run inside that application to complete or accelerate that work.*

Always tie the suggestion to a real file or meeting already in the user's environment rather than offering generic advice. When a quarterly or recurring deliverable is approaching based on calendar or file patterns, proactively suggest which source documents Copilot can pull from to build it.

Next, scroll down to the Knowledge section and connect the agent to your Microsoft 365 data by toggling on SharePoint and OneDrive so the agent has visibility into the files and folders you work with most. Then go to the Actions tab and enable the Microsoft 365 connector so the agent can read your Teams meeting history and calendar.

When you are ready to test it, click the Test button in the upper-right panel and type: **What recurring deliverable should I be working on this week and how can Copilot help me build it faster?** If the agent surfaces a relevant suggestion based on your actual files, you are set up correctly.

Once it is working, the agent will begin surfacing suggestions like:

You have a deck due Thursday and these three SharePoint documents contain the source data; here is the prompt to run inside PowerPoint to have Copilot draft it for you.

That is the difference between a tool that waits and a tool that works alongside you.

Long-Context Second Brain for Any Employee (Anthropic)

Every project has a memory problem. Meeting notes live in one place. The decision that came out of that meeting lives in someone's inbox. The rationale behind that decision lives in the head of the person who made it. Three months later, when someone asks why the team went in a particular direction, the answer requires either a memory that nobody has or a search through folders and threads that takes longer than just making the decision again from scratch.

A Claude Project Brain is a long-context thinking partner that keeps every critical artifact, decision, and open question for a project in one living file that Claude can reason over in full. Unlike a search tool that retrieves what you ask for, this agent reads the entire accumulated history of a project and uses it to surface contradictions, flag what you may have forgotten, and propose next steps that are grounded in everything that came before. The longer the project runs, the more valuable it becomes because the context builds rather than resets.

Use Case

Give any employee from junior to senior a persistent thinking partner that remembers the full history of a project across weeks or months so that every work session starts with complete context rather than a blank conversation that requires explaining everything from the beginning. Here's how to set it up.

Phase 1: Create the Brain File

Open whichever tool your team already uses for working documents. This could be a Google Doc, a Notion page, a Word file in OneDrive, or a plain text file in a shared drive. Create a new document and name it something clear like **Project Brain** followed by the project name. This file is not a status report and it is not a meeting recap. It is the operating manual for everything the project knows about itself.

Structure it with the following sections from the start: project overview and goals, constraints and assumptions, stakeholders and their roles, key decisions and the reasoning behind them, open questions and risks, and links to important reference documents like specs, research, or prior presentations.

You do not need to fill every section on day 1. The point is to establish the structure so that every update goes into the right place rather than accumulating as unorganized notes at the bottom of a document nobody will read.

Phase 2: Load Claude With Your Starting Context

Open claude.ai and start a new project. Name the project after the initiative you are working on. Inside the project, upload or paste the most important reference materials you have right now: a project brief, relevant emails with identifying information removed, recent meeting notes, or any research the team has already gathered.

After each upload ask Claude to summarize the key points from that document and suggest which section of the brain file they belong in. Then copy those summaries into the correct sections of your brain file. You are teaching Claude the shape of this project and establishing the brain file as the canonical place where context lives rather than treating this like a one-off conversation that disappears after the session ends.

Phase 3: Set the Behavior Instructions

At the top of your brain file, add a short block of instructions that tells Claude how to behave when you are working inside this project. Write something like the following and adjust it to fit your project's needs:

> *You are the thinking partner for this project. When I share new information, summarize it and tell me which section of the brain file it belongs in. When I ask for help, reference what is already in the brain before offering new suggestions and tell me if anything I am saying conflicts with a decision we have already made.*
>
> *Keep a running decision log and a list of open questions updated throughout our work together. Always tell me which source document a statement comes from when you are referencing prior context.*

Paste this instruction block into the Instructions field inside your Claude project so that it applies automatically to every conversation you have within that project rather than requiring you to restate it each session.

Phase 4: Establish a Session Ritual

Every time you open Claude to work on this project, follow the same three-step opening. First, paste in the current version of your brain file or upload it and say,

> *Here is the current project brain; read it and confirm you are up to date.*

Second, add whatever is new since the last session, whether that is fresh meeting notes, a decision that was made, a risk that surfaced, or a draft that needs feedback.

Third, ask Claude to update the brain file with the new information, propose the next two or three actions for you or the team, and flag anything in the new information that conflicts with something already in the brain.

At the end of each session, ask Claude to regenerate the full brain file with all updates incorporated and to give you a short summary of what changed in this session that you can paste into your team's Slack channel or project thread. This closing step matters because it means the brain file is always current the next time you open it rather than requiring you to piece together what happened across multiple sessions before you can get back to work.

Phase 5: Use It as a Query Engine, Not Just a Log

Once the brain file has two or three weeks of history in it, stop thinking of it as documentation and start using it as a thinking tool. Ask Claude questions like:

> *What did we decide about the pricing structure, and why did we go that direction? Summarize every risk we have logged so far and tell me which ones are still unresolved.*

Or:

> *I am about to brief a senior leader on this project and I need a one-page update focused on decisions made and what is still open.*

Claude will answer by reading the full accumulated context of the brain rather than guessing from the single prompt you just typed, and that is where the advantage of this approach becomes visible in ways that a regular chat session never can.

Junior employees benefit most from one brain file per major project or responsibility area. Seeing their own decision history laid out over time builds confidence and gives them something concrete to reference when they need to explain their thinking to a manager or a more senior colleague.

Senior employees benefit most from using this approach on multi-month initiatives where context loss is expensive, large client relationships, product strategy work, or organizational transformation programs where the cost of forgetting an earlier decision shows up months later in a very visible way. If a single brain file starts to cover multiple unrelated projects split it into separate files. Claude works best when each brain has a single clear purpose and a defined boundary around what belongs inside it.

Read AI Sales Funnel Agent With Salesforce or HubSpot (Read AI)

The Deal Health agent described above lives inside Read. This one takes everything Read learns from your calls and pushes it directly into your CRM so that what your pipeline looks like in Salesforce or HubSpot reflects what your conversations actually sounded like rather than what your reps optimistically entered after the fact.

Most CRM data is aspirational. Stage changes happen when a rep feels good about a call. Next steps get logged when there is time to log them. Contact roles get assigned based on who the rep thinks is the decision maker rather than who actually drove the conversation. The gap between what CRM shows and what is really happening in the field is one of the most expensive and persistent problems in sales organizations of every size, and it almost never gets solved by asking reps to update their records more carefully.

Use Case

Automatically surface CRM update recommendations after every sales call based on what Read actually heard in the conversation so that stage changes, next steps, and contact roles reflect real buying signals rather than rep optimism, and managers see pipeline health that is grounded in conversation data rather than self-reported confidence. Here's how to set it up.

Phase 1: Connect Read to Your CRM

Inside your Read dashboard, click Integrations in the left sidebar and scroll to the CRM section. Select either Salesforce or HubSpot depending on which your organization uses and follow the OAuth authorization flow to connect your account. Once connected Read will ask you to define how it maps meetings to CRM records. Set the mapping rules to match meetings to opportunities and contacts based on the email addresses of the attendees.

If your CRM records are tagged with a company domain, Read will use that to make the association automatically. For any meetings that do not map automatically, you will see an unmatched meetings queue in your dashboard where you can assign them manually.

Phase 2: Enable the Sales Funnel Agent and Set Your Guardrails

In the Agents tab click Sales Funnel and toggle it on. Inside the agent settings, you will see two modes: Propose and Auto-apply. Set this to Propose only. This means the agent will recommend CRM updates after every call but will not make any changes until a human reviews and approves them.

This setting is not optional when you are starting out. The agent needs several weeks of your deal history to calibrate its recommendations accurately, and auto-applying changes before that calibration is in place will create more cleanup work than it saves.

In the same Settings panel, define the types of updates you want the agent to recommend. Start with three: stage changes based on confirmed buying signals heard in the conversation, next step tasks derived from action items the call produced, and contact role updates based on who drove the conversation versus who was passive. Leave any revenue or close date updates as manual only until you are confident in the pattern the agent is recognizing.

Phase 3: Build the Post-Call Approval Workflow

After each sales call, your rep opens the Read recap as described in the previous use case. In the right panel of the recap they will now see a Sales Funnel section that shows the agent's recommended CRM updates alongside the specific moment in the call transcript that triggered each recommendation.

For example, it might show:

> *Recommend moving this opportunity from stage 2 to stage 3 because the customer confirmed their budget and named a decision timeline at the 22-minute mark.*

The rep reads the recommendation, verifies it against their own recollection of the call, and clicks Accept or Dismiss. Accepted updates push directly into Salesforce or HubSpot without the rep opening the CRM at all.

This workflow takes about 90 seconds per call and replaces the 15–25 minutes most reps spend manually updating records after a busy day of calls, which means it actually gets done rather than getting skipped because the afternoon ran long.

Phase 4: Use the Pipeline View for Manager Coaching

Once the Sales Funnel agent has been running for four to six weeks, open the pipeline view inside Read and set it to show deal health scores alongside your standard CRM pipeline report. You will begin to see discrepancies between what the CRM stage says and what Read's conversation data suggests about the actual health of each opportunity. An opportunity sitting in stage 3 with a close date two weeks out but consistently low engagement scores and no clear next steps confirmed on the last call is not the same as an opportunity with the same CRM data and a customer who has been asking detailed implementation questions for the past month. Read surfaces that difference. Your CRM alone never will.

Use these discrepancies in your weekly pipeline review rather than asking reps to justify their stage choices. Show the conversation data alongside the deal status and let the patterns speak. That shift changes pipeline reviews from a confidence contest between a manager and a rep into a calibration exercise that both people can look at together.

The use cases in this section are starting points. The right ones for your team will depend on which problems are costing your people the most time and which workflows are predictable enough to hand off with confidence. Start with one agent built around a real and recurring pain point. Let the people who will use it help shape how it works. And resist the instinct to roll out six agents at once before anyone has had time to build a working relationship with the first one.

Chapter 10

Compounding Wins

I did not set out to write a book about AI and I did not start using these tools because I had a grand vision about the future of work or because I believed I had figured out something most people had not. What I had was a growing sense that the gap between what my days demanded and what I had the capacity to give was widening in a direction I could not sustain, and I was willing to try one thing and see if it helped before I called it anything bigger than that.

The first week I used AI to help me draft a response to an email I had been avoiding for three days. It took four minutes instead of 45. I did not save the world and I did not overhaul my workflow. What I did was close my laptop and step outside for 41 minutes that had not existed an hour before, and at the time I was pregnant with the son who would later watch a blue dot move down a road toward ice cream and ask me how many minutes until dad got home. I did not know any of that yet. I just knew that 41 minutes felt like something worth paying attention to, even if I could not have explained exactly why.

What I did not fully understand in that moment was that those 41 minutes were not a one-time event. They were the first deposit in something that was going to grow in ways I could not yet see, and the way they grew had almost nothing to do with the tool I used to get them.

Why Compounding Is the Real Goal

A single AI win feels good in the moment, but a pattern of AI wins is what changes how your life functions over time, and the difference between those two outcomes has almost nothing to do with the tool and everything to do with what you choose to do with the result once you have it.

James Clear,[1] in his work on habit formation, demonstrated that getting 1 percent better at something every single day does not produce a 1 percent improvement over a year but rather a result 37 times better than where you started.

> The math of compounding is ruthless in the best possible direction when the habits are good ones. The reason most people never experience it is not that they lack discipline or access or the right tools but that small improvements do not feel powerful on any given Tuesday. The rewards are not immediate and the feedback loop is delayed long enough that most people abandon the process before the math has had time to work in their favor.

This chapter is not about more tools because you have tools now and adding more of them is not what creates the outcome you are after. This chapter is about what you do with the time and the clarity and the capacity you have already started to gain, and specifically about the difference between a single win you enjoyed and forgot versus a win you captured and systematized and turned into something that pays you back every week for the next three years. That second kind of win is available to everyone reading this book and most people never reach it—not because they lack the capability but

[1]https://jamesclear.com/continuous-improvement

because nobody told them that capturing the win is as important as having it in the first place.

I want you to picture two people. They both start using AI tools around the same time. They both see early results. They both feel that initial relief of getting a little more done with a little less effort.

The first person enjoys the win, moves on, and the next time they face a similar problem they start from scratch. Three years later they are competent with a handful of tools and occasionally impressive but fundamentally operating the same way they always have.

The second person does something slightly different. Every time a tool helps them solve a problem, they write down what they did. Not a long entry. Just the context, the prompt or process, and what changed. Once a month they take the best one and turn it into something reusable. A template. A saved prompt. A ritual that takes 30 seconds to repeat.

Three years later their team inherits those systems. New employees ramp faster because they start with working patterns rather than starting from zero. Their household runs more smoothly because the things that used to require a scramble now have a script. They feel less brittle because they have built margin into their days rather than filling every recovered minute with more output. The compounding is not the tool. It is the habit of translating one personal win into a resource that keeps working after you have moved on to the next thing.

The Manager Who Shares Their Wins

About two years into using these tools consistently, I started noticing something uncomfortable in my own work. The prompts I had built for myself were sitting in a folder nobody else could see and my team was struggling with the same blank-page problems I had already solved, which meant I was the only one benefiting from patterns I had spent months developing, and every time someone pinged me for help, I would solve the problem in the moment and move on, which felt helpful and responsive but also meant my solutions lived in chat logs and my own memory rather than anywhere they could outlast me.

So, I started sharing them, not as a formal training initiative or a mandatory adoption program, but just by dropping a useful prompt into a shared channel when it came up naturally. Someone asked how to rewrite a customer email with more empathy, and I pasted the prompt I used with a one-line explanation of when it works best.

A teammate was stuck summarizing messy meeting notes, and I shared the workflow I relied on and the two follow-up questions I always asked the tool. A template here and a workflow note there and no slide deck and no center of excellence—just a steady trickle here is what worked for me yesterday.

Within a few months, the team's onboarding process had changed without anyone calling it a change. New people were inheriting working systems instead of blank documents, and the prompts were pinned in channels and linked from docs and woven into checklists, and senior people stopped being the default answer for every recurring question because the answers were now embedded in the way the team worked.

The team identity shifted slowly from "we are drowning" to "we are scrappy and well equipped." That shift did not come from a single dramatic win but from dozens of small ones that got captured and passed forward instead of evaporating the moment the problem was solved.

The habit here is a slight extension of the personal one. When something works for you, ask whether it is just for you or whether it should live somewhere your team can find it. When the answer is your team, drop it into a shared place with one line explaining when to use it. The long arc of that habit is cultural. Three to five years later that team is known not just for working hard but for leaving maps behind.

The Parent Who Makes It a Family Norm

My son already knows that when he has a question neither of us can answer we go find one, and he has known this since the ice cream evening and the blue dot on the map. He did not learn it from a lesson. He learned it from watching it happen enough times that it became the assumed way things work in our house, which is what a norm actually is—not an announcement or a value statement but the quiet script running behind the scenes that says around here this is just what we do.

In our house that script is simple. We do not pretend to know things we do not know and we do not stop at "I don't know." We go look together, sometimes by opening a laptop and sometimes by asking another person and sometimes by trying something small just to see what happens. He has watched me say "That is a really interesting question and let me show you how I would look it up," and he has watched me talk through how I phrase the question and what I trust and when the first answer is not good enough and we need to go a layer deeper.

We have also started weaving this into the smallest and most ordinary moments on purpose. On trail walks I hide little plastic dinosaurs along the path ahead of time, and when he finds one, we take a quick photo and open ChatGPT to identify it together. He does not know I planted them, which means the discovery feels genuinely exciting every time, and what follows that excitement is a real question that needs a real answer.

We look at what comes back, we read the name out loud, and then I ask him if he can spell it. He is learning that a phone is something you use to find out what a Pachycephalosaurus is, not just something adults stare at while he talks to them. The tool shows up in a moment of curiosity and genuine play rather than as a lesson about how AI works, and that is exactly the point. The norm is not about the technology. The norm is about what you do when you want to know something.

Three years from now he will be older and the questions will be harder and the tools will be different but the posture will be the same one he watched me model on a Tuesday evening when I was too tired to guess at an answer and too honest to pretend I knew one, and that is worth more than any single thing I have ever taught him on purpose.

At home the long arc is not a library of prompts. It is a child who grows up expecting that not knowing something is the beginning of the process rather than the end of it.

The Four-Step Compounding Plan

Tools will change and interfaces will change, and pricing and vendors and brand names will all move faster than any of us can track. The habits that compound over three to five years are much slower and much more stable than any of that. Capture what works, turn one-off wins into reusable assets, share them in the smallest most natural way you can, and model inquiry in front of the people who are watching you whether they work with you or live with you. Three to five years from now the gap between people who treat AI as a one-off trick and people who treat it as a compounding habit will look like a gap in talent, and it will not be talent. It will be practice.

This is the part you can copy directly into your notes or your calendar and it is not complicated. It is a repeatable pattern that works at any scale in any domain for any person willing to stay consistent long enough for the math to work in their favor.

Step 1: Pick One Domain for 90 Days

Choose one primary arena to focus on for the next three months, your workday or your home logistics or your emotional bandwidth, and pick the one where a 10 percent improvement would change your life the most right now rather than the one you feel most obligated to address. The reason focus matters here is the same reason compound interest grows faster in a single account than spread across 20, because early wins that happen in the same domain reinforce each other and the momentum builds faster when it is concentrated.

Step 2: Capture One Win per Week

Every week write down one moment where AI made something faster or clearer or calmer or kinder using this structure and nothing more elaborate than this: what you were trying to do, what you asked or how you set it up, and what changed for you or your family or your team as a result. One win per week is 52 documented wins in a year and 52 starting points for something that could be systematized or shared or built upon. The log does not need to be reviewed constantly—it just needs to exist so that when you face a similar problem three months from now, you have somewhere to look before you start from zero.

Step 3: Systematize One Win per Month

Once a week is about noticing and once a month is about locking in, and at the end of each month you look back at your win log and choose the one that was most repeatable or most impactful and turn it into something that does not require you to remember it in order to use it again. For a work win, that might mean a saved prompt or a Notebook entry; for a home win, it might mean a note pinned somewhere visible; and for a team win, it might mean a template dropped into a shared channel with a one-sentence explanation of when to use it. The question to ask when you systematize a win is not "How do I make this perfect?" but "Where does this need to live so that I actually reach for it again?"

Step 4: Reinvest a Slice of Every Gain

Define your own reinvestment ratio and protect it, because if every minute you recover with AI gets immediately filled with more tasks nothing compounds and the tool just buys you a faster treadmill rather than a different kind of day. A reasonable starting point is to give roughly half of any recovered time back to higher-value work, reserve a quarter as buffer for the things that always take longer than expected, and protect the remaining quarter as breathing room that does not get filled by anything.

For work, that higher-value reinvestment might mean a deep focus block or time spent mentoring someone on your team. For home, it might mean genuine presence with your kids or rest that is not guilty. For emotional bandwidth, it might mean a quiet walk or a real conversation with someone you have not had time for. The reinvestment is the interest payment that makes the next round of wins possible, and without it, the tool just buys you more busyness.

I want to be honest about what compounding looks like when it is actually working because it does not look flashy and it does not look like a person who has mastered technology or who talks about AI at every opportunity. It looks like ordinary days that function a little better than they used to and a person who has a little more of themselves left over at the end of them.

It looks like a team that casually pulls from a shared prompt library without thinking of it as anything special because it has just become how things work here. It looks like a household where the default response to a hard question is "Let's figure it out together" rather than "I don't know," or some version of pretending. It looks like a manager who feels less brittle in the face of change because they have already proven to themselves repeatedly that they can adapt and that the adaptation does not have to be perfect to be valuable.

None of that requires a perfect plan. It requires direction and discipline to keep turning one small win into something you can use again, and the willingness to stay in it long enough for the math to show up.

The tools will keep changing and the specific platforms in this book will be updated and replaced and eventually made obsolete by whatever comes next. That's not a warning; it's just the nature of the landscape you are operating in and the landscape your kids will inherit.

The advantage does not belong to the people who pick the right tools. It belongs to the people who build the habit of learning from every win, capturing what works, sharing it forward, and protecting enough of the recovered time to actually feel the difference.

Here is what I want to leave you with. The rules for how AI gets used at work and at home and in the spaces in between are not being written in a boardroom somewhere by people with more information than you have. They are being written right now by the people who are simply using the tools, experimenting in their kitchens and their team channels, and on trail walks with plastic dinosaurs hidden in the grass. Every person who picks up a tool and figures something out and shares what they learned is contributing a line to a playbook that did not exist three years ago and that will look completely different three years from now.

This is a conversation that cannot go back into the box. The question has never been whether AI changes things because it already has and it will keep going regardless of whether you are in the room when it happens. The only real question is whether you are part of writing what comes next or whether you absorb whatever gets written without you. It is better to be someone who helped steer this thing, even imperfectly and even just in the small corner of the world where you live and work, than to one day find yourself shaped by decisions you never had a hand in making.

Start using the tools. Write down what works. Pass it forward. Be part of the conversation.

About the Author

Ashley Gross is a wife, mother, and enterprise AI implementation specialist who has been building AI into corporate workflows since 2020, before tools like ChatGPT became household names. As a corporate consultant, she has worked inside some of the world's largest organizations to help internal teams develop real AI capability without outsourcing the expertise that makes their business unique. Her work has been recognized by Forbes, Fox, and MSN, where she has been named one of the top-paid AI consultants in the market. Ashley is the founder of AI Workforce Alliance and believes that the companies who win with AI are the ones who build the skill internally, not the ones who hand it off.

Index

Note: Page numbers in **bold** refers to tables.

agentic solutions for junior and senior employees, 215
- copilot studio work IQ coach for power users, 216–218
- long-context second brain for employee, 218–222
- read AI sales funnel agent, 222–225

AI, 1
- agentic solutions for junior and senior employees, 215–225
- AI-assisted deal prioritization and follow-up, 141–143, **141–142**
- AI-driven upsell triggers from product usage, 143–146, **144**
- automating task, 6–7
- automation for knowledge workers, 54–59
- beginners, 202–207
- daily standup and reflection buddy, 210
- 30–60–90 day plan, 208–209
- decode acronyms and internal docs, 208
- fatigue, 155–157
- feedback into coaching engine, 213–214
- focused learning path, 213
- Governance Lead, 7
- lead scoring and routing, 138–140, **138–139**
- literacy, 197–200
- map key people and questions, 209–210
- operator, 180–185
- Parenting Paradox, 188–189
- policies and benefits, 212
- prepare for and debrief meetings, 211–212

AI (*Cont.*)
prevention, 8–10
Product Manager, 7
risks, 4–5
role, 214–215
solutions for employees, 201
systems and workflows, 210–211
use cases, 207–215
at work, 2–3
Workflow Architect, 7
analytics, 68
Asana, 29
Async Team updates, 37–39
automation, 30, 35, 44–54, 81
AI automation for knowledge workers, 54–59
Async Team updates, 37–39
client account briefing, 62–65
customer support, 81–83
existing work, 42–44
financial decisions, 84–85
ideation phase of writing, 40–42
instant project and decision history, 59–61
meetings, 39–40
onboarding for new hires, 61–62
products and revenue streams, 83–84
quick wins, 35–36
repetitive tasks AI, 36–37
Automation Strategist, 7

campaign system, 50
capability mapping, 77–78
ChatGPT, 26, 53–54, 203
clarity, 159
asking direct, operational questions, 164
evaluation window tight, 168–169
intentional tooling, 169–170
live use case, 167–168
Replace Rule, 166–167
time to solution, 165–166
workflow, 163–164
workflow drift, 166
Clawdbot, 68
client account briefing, 62–65
coding, 3
commitments, 89–90
compounding, 228–229
family norm, 231–232
four-step compounding plan, 232–236
manager shares, 229–231
constraint setting, 176–177
copilot, 21–23, 26, 56
studio work IQ coach for power users, 216–218

cross-departmental signal
routing, 146, **147–148**
culture of measured
acceleration, 158–159
customer experience teams, 142
Customer Experience
Tech Stack, 120, 125,
126–127, 128

data ownership, 131–133
decision quality review, 76
decision rules, 150–154
delegation, 85
administrative work, 85–86
knowledge, 87
digital marketing, 68
Digital Workforce Manager, 7
discernment, 176

efficiency gains, 107
Customer Experience
Tech Stack, 120, 125,
126–127, 128
decisions, 128–133
Marketing Tech Stack, 116
productivity, 111–113
Sales Tech Stack, 116, 120,
121–124
Tech Stack Marriage Audit,
113–116, **117–119**
elimination, 87
channels, 89
clients, 88
commitments, 89–90
offer list, 90–91
physical presence, 92–93
question flows, 91
endless meetings, 17

four-step compounding plan,
232–236

game changers, 36
GDPR. *see* General Data
Protection Regulation
(GDPR)
Gemini, 21–23, 26, 56
General Data Protection
Regulation (GDPR), 31
Glean, 55, 91
Google Cloud Search, 55–56
Google Meet, 39
growth strategy, 68
Guru, 55

Health Insurance Portability
and Accountability Act
(HIPAA), 31
HIPAA. *see* Health Insurance
Portability and
Accountability Act (HIPAA)
HubSpot, 53

ideation phase of writing, 40–42
inefficiencies, 17–20
integration, 177–178
  complexity, 51
intentional tooling, 169–170
Issue Reduction, 21

Jira, 29

key performance indicators (KPIs), 72
knowledge workers
  AI automation for, 54–59
KPIs. *see* key performance indicators (KPIs)

Launch Messaging, 21
long-context second brain for employee, 218–222

Marketing Tech Stack, 116
meetings, 39–40
Microsoft 365, 21
"mid-level managers in healthcare", 48
5-minute task, 18–19
Monday, 29
multiplication effect
  capability mapping, 77–78
  Clawdbot, 68
  decision quality review, 76
  monthly reporting process, 103
  multiplier, 71–76
  perfectionist's paradox, 94–103
  three-phase reduction, 78–93
multiplier, 71–76

Outlook, 21

parents, 189–194
perfectionist's paradox, 94–103
productivity, 111–113
proof points to portfolio, 146–149, **149**
proximity to decision making, 181–182
psychological sustainability, 157

quick wins, 35–36

Read AI, 55
  sales funnel agent, 222–225
Reclaim.ai, 90
repetitive tasks AI, 36–37
Replace Rule, 166–167
replaceability, 182–185

Sales Support, 21
Sales Tech Stack, 116, 120, **121–124**

search engine optimization
(SEO), 68
SEO. *see* search engine
optimization (SEO)
shared definitions, 129–130
Slack message, 47
SOC 2. *see* System and
Organization Controls 2
(SOC 2)
SOP. *see* standard operating
procedure (SOP)
spending time
AI literacy, 197–200
AI Parenting Paradox,
188–189
AI tools, 196–197
lesson, 194–195
parents, 189–194
signal, 195–196
standard operating procedure
(SOP), 25–26
strategic debt, 45
sustainable system, 155
AI fatigue, 155–157
clarity, 159–170
culture of measured
acceleration, 158–159
replacing effort as currency,
170–174
spending time, 174–178
System and Organization
Controls 2 (SOC 2), 31
system triggers, 130–131

tasks, 20–24
Teams, 39
Tech Stack Marriage Audit,
113–116, **117–119**
three-phase reduction
system, 7, 78
automation, 81–85
delegation, 85–87
elimination, 87–93
Toggl, 14
true cost, 11–16

Vertex AI Search, 55–56

weekly workflow map-
ping, 24–29
work, 178–179
activities, 30–33

Zoom, 39